D0349180

A Handbook of Coins
of the British Isles

(*top to bottom*) Maundy Fourpence of 1670 (reverse); Maundy Threepence of 1691 (reverse); Maundy Fourpence of 1953 (reverse); Maundy Threepence of 1953 (reverse): and × 2

A HANDBOOK OF COINS OF THE BRITISH ISLES

by

Howard W. Bradley

ROBERT HALE · LONDON

© Howard W. Bradley 1978 and 1982
First published in Great Britain 1978
Second edition 1982

ISBN 0 7090 0652 7

Robert Hale Limited
Clerkenwell House
Clerkenwell Green
London, EC1.

Printed
in Great Britain by
REDWOOD BURN LIMITED
Trowbridge, Wiltshire
and bound by Western Book Co.

Contents

Acknowledgments

I should like to thank Mr R. A. Gardner and the Department of Coins and Medals at the British Museum for supplying the photographic reproductions of coins in this book. My thanks are also due to the ABC Historic Publications for allowing me to use information in the 1982 edition of *Museums and Galleries* in compiling the list of museums which have coins and medals. Acknowledgment is also made to the Birmingham Mint Ltd, The Danbury Mint, The Franklin Mint of Pennsylvania, the IMI Kynoch Mint and the Pobjoy Mint for supplying information for the entry on mints. I also wish to thank the Bank of England for the information on the laws regarding the exchange of gold bullion and gold coin.

A

ABBEY CROWN This was the name given to the gold crowns struck at the Holyrood Palace Mint during the reigns of James V and Mary of Scotland in the sixteenth century. The crown produced for James V circulated at 20s. (£1). The obverse depicted a Scottish shield crowned with a saltire cross (Cross of St Andrew) to the left and to the right surrounded by the legend IACOBVS 5 DEI GRA. REX SCOTORVM. The reverse showed a cross fleury with thistles in the angles and the inscription PER LIGNVM CRVCIS SALVI SVMVS ("By the wood of the cross are we saved"). On later types this Biblical quotation was changed to CRVCIS ARMA SEQVAMVR ("Let us follow the arms of the cross").

The Abbey crowns struck during the reign of Mary were almost identical in appearance to the later types of her father except for a trefoil replacing the cross on either side of the shield and the obvious change in the royal titles on the obverse.

When this denomination was issued in the reign of Mary, its value had risen to 22s. (£1.10p.) but the weight remained the same at $52\frac{1}{4}$ grains. A new lighter coin called a twenty shillings was struck at the old value.

ANGEL The gold angel first struck in 1465 during the reign of Edward IV became the longest surviving and most widely used late medieval coin, and was accepted as currency in other European countries. Until 1489 and the re-organization of the nation's coinage by Henry VII, the angel and its half were in fact the only gold coins produced.

The angel was introduced because the noble (*q.v.*) had been discontinued after being revalued to the unwieldy amount of 8s. 4d. ($41\frac{1}{2}$p.) and the king decided that it would be wise to continue striking coins at the old value of one-third of a pound. The noble had been worth 6s. 8d. ($33\frac{1}{2}$p.), which was the usual professional fee at the time. The value of the angel was one of the main reasons for its popularity, for it was very convenient to have a coin circulating at the rate of half a mark (a money of account) and a third of a pound.

The angel weighed only 80 grains as opposed to the 108 grains of the noble. It retained the same weight until the second coinage of James I in 1604 when it was reduced to 71 grains. It was later reduced to $65\frac{1}{2}$ grains (1619) and $64\frac{3}{4}$ grains (1625). During the period of stable weight until 1604, the angel had, in fact, been rising in value. Henry VIII revalued it at 7s. 6d. ($37\frac{1}{2}$p.) in 1526 and 8s. (40p.) in 1544 and introduced the George noble (*q.v.*) at 6s. 8d. Edward VI, in his attempt to stabilize the monetary system after the extravagances of his father, raised its value to 10s. (50p.) and, apart from a brief revaluation to 11s. (55p.) from 1611–19, the angel was current at the same rate until it was discontinued in 1634.

1. Angel of 1465 (obverse and reverse)

The obverse of the first angel showed the Archangel Michael slaying the dragon (hence its name) and the legend EDWARD DI. GRA. REX ANGL. Z FRANC. DNS. IB. The reverse bore a ship with the royal arms on the hull surmounted by a cross and the sun above (the latter was omitted on later issues). On either side of the cross was a small sun to the right and a Yorkist rose to the left. This central motif replaced the figure of the king clad in full armour, carrying a sword and a shield and standing in a ship, which had been used on the noble. The reverse legend was PER CRVCEM TVAM SALVA NOS XRC REDEMPTOR ("By Thy cross save us, O Christ our redeemer").

The half-angel or angelet was struck almost as frequently as the angel and had a similar design. However, the reverse legend was shorter and for early issues read O CRVX AVE SPES VNICA ("Hail, O Cross, our only hope"). The half-angel was last struck in the second coinage of James I and was discontinued in 1619. At certain short periods during the reigns of Henry VIII, Elizabeth I and James I, quarter-angels were also issued.

Angels were popular coins with the general public for more than just reasons of convenience. Coins of later dates are often found with a hole punched through the centre. They were most probably used as touch pieces (*q.v.*). Medalets with a pierced hole, resembling angels, were also produced during the reign of Charles II for use as touch pieces.

ANGELET   This is another name for the half-angel. See ANGEL.

ANGL.   This abbreviation, A., ANG., or ANGLIE for the Latin ANGLIAE was used in conjunction with the word REX for the title of King of England. Upon James I's accession to the throne in 1604, the letters SCO. or SC. for *Scotiae* (Scotland) were added. This title was changed to MAG. BRIT. REX (*q.v.*) for the second coinage which appeared in the same year. The same ANG. SCO. legend was used on Cromwell's pattern crowns except that it was preceded by R.P., the abbreviation for *republica*, and the title PRO., protector, replaced REX.

REX ANGLOR or REX ANGLORVM (King of the English) had been used since Saxon times. Earlier titles of the Saxon kings were REX TO. B. (*totae Britanniae* – all Britain), SAXON-IORVM, SAXONVM (the Saxons), or OCCIDENTALIVM (the west of England or Wessex, where the Saxons lived).

ANGLO-GALLIC COINS   This term is used for those coins struck by the English kings for their French possessions from the reign of Henry II (1154–89) to that of Henry VIII (1509–47). The first coins of Henry II were silver deniers and oboles and the last to be issued were groats, from 1513 to 1518.

The early Norman kings did not issue separate coins for the Duchy of Normandy. During the period when the English held possessions across the Channel, they were at various times over-lords of the territories of Aquitaine, Poitou, Guienne, Gascony and Normandy. Most of the coinage had ceased by 1451 when England had lost all her land in France with the exception of Calais, which was finally relinquished in 1558 during the reign of Mary.

Henry II acquired Poitou and the Duchy of Aquitaine on his marriage to the Duchess Eleanor in 1152 and when he became king two years later he struck his first coins especially for these territories. It was not until the reign of Edward II (1327–77) that other silver denominations and new gold pieces were introduced. From that time a variety of denominations, with their fractions, was issued. They included:

IN GOLD:

angelot – struck by Henry VI, valued at two thirds of a salute (see below).

chaise or écu – first struck by Edward III and so called from the reverse design of the ruler sitting on a throne and similar to coins of the French King Philip VI (1328–50).

florin – first struck by Edward III; like his English coin an imitation of the Florentine piece.

guiennois – first struck by Edward III; King standing under a gothic portico.

hardi d'or – first struck by Edward, the Black Prince.

leopard – first struck by Edward III; like its English counterpart so called because of the leopard on the obverse.

mouton – first struck by Henry V and so called because of the Easter lamb on the obverse.

pavillon – first struck by the Black Prince; like a similar coin of Philip VI of Valois, so called because of the king under a canopy or tent.

salute – first struck by Henry V; so called because of the obverse design showing the annunciation or salutation of Mary.

IN SILVER:

blanc – two types, *gros* or *grand blanc* and *petit blanc* of groats struck by Henry VI.

hardi d'argent – first struck by Edward III; a copy of coins of French kings with the monarch holding a sword. The name is thought to have been derived from a king of France, Philip le Hardi.

sterling – first struck by Edward III; similar to English pennies.

tresin – a coin valued at three deniers struck by Henry VI.

ANGLO-HANOVERIAN COINS This is applied to the *pfennig, groschen, gulden* and *talers* issued by the early Hanoverian kings (George I to William IV) who retained their German possessions of Brunswick, Lüneburg and Hanover. Salic law prevented them from passing to Queen Victoria and the new ruler in 1837 was the Duke of Cumberland (see CUMBERLAND JACKS).

The obverses of the so-called Anglo-Hanoverian coins showed either the king's portrait or his monogram and the reverse the British royal coat of arms and the value.

AQT. AQVT. In connection with the words DVX (duke) or DNS (*dominus,* or lord), these abbreviations for AQVITANIAE appeared in the legend of English coins from the reign of Edward I (1272–1307) until the beginning of the fifteenth century and referred to the monarch's claim to the French territory of Aquitaine. The title DVX appeared prior to 1360, DNS afterwards.

See also ANGLO-GALLIC COINS.

ARMSTRONG FARTHING In 1660 Sir Thomas Armstrong received the licence from Charles II to mint copper farthings for use in Ireland. However, it is thought that very few, if any, actually circulated there as the Governor of Ireland prohibited the issue. The obverse showed a crown and two sceptres, the reverse a crowned harp. The legend on the obverse read CAROLUS 11 D.G. M.B. and was continued on the reverse with FRA. ET HIB. REX.

B

BALANCE HALF MERK This Scottish silver coin contained seven-eighths pure silver and weighed $71\frac{1}{3}$ grains. It was valued at 6s. 8d. ($33\frac{1}{2}$p.) and was issued by James VI from 1591 to 1593. It was so-called because the reverse showed a pair of scales superimposed on an upright sword. The legend was a comment on the design it encircled, namely HIS DIFFERT REGE TYRANNVS ("In these a tyrant differs from a king"). The obverse with the King's titles displayed a crowned Scottish shield flanked by two thistles.

2. Balance Half Merk (reverse)

Balance quarter merks with a similar design were issued at the same period.

BANK OF ENGLAND TOKENS See DOLLAR, EIGHTEEN PENCE, NINEPENCE, THREE-SHILLING PIECE.

BANK OF IRELAND TOKENS See FIVE PENCE, TEN PENCE, THIRTY PENCE, SIX-SHILLING PIECE.

BARBAROUS RADIATES As a result of her political and economic troubles in the third and fourth centuries, Rome failed to send enough coins to her British colony. Therefore copies of *antoniniani* of contemporary Roman emperors were struck in Britain. These imitations are commonly known as barbarous radiates because of the poor workmanship and the fact that the emperor wears a radiate crown instead of a laurel wreath.

BAWBEE The bawbee was a Scottish billon coin containing only a quarter of its weight in silver. It was first struck by James

V in 1538 at his Edinburgh and Stirling mints. The same king also minted a half- and a quarter-bawbee but only the larger fraction was struck for his daughter Mary. The bawbee was worth six Scottish pennies or one English halfpenny.

The obverse of the bawbee depicted a crowned thistle and the reverse a saltire cross with a *fleur-de-lis* in the two side angles. On one of Mary's issues the latter showed a cross potent with a cross in each angle.

The minting of the bawbee was suspended until 1677, when it reappeared as a copper coin bearing the portrait of Charles II on the obverse and a crowned thistle on the reverse. Production of the bawbee with a similar design was continued during the reigns of William and Mary and William II (William III of England).

3. Bawbee of James V (obverse and reverse)

The origin of the name is uncertain. Some consider bawbee a corruption of the French *bas pièce* or *bas billon*, others think it is derived from Alexander Orrok, the Laird of Sillebawbie, a one time Master of the Scottish mint, and said to be the first to strike the denomination. At times the coin was called a 'babie' because of the similarity to its name and its small size. In 1693 it was recorded by the Presbytery of Lanark that a collection one contained "two bad shillings, a thrie, and a babie".

BEZANT   A bezant was a gold *solidus* named after the city of Byzantium, and circulated from the fourth to the fourteenth century in most countries of Europe, including England.

BILLON   The metal used as a substitute for silver in debased silver currencies was copper and the name given to the alloy was billon.

BLACK FARTHING   This term, or 'black money', was used to describe the first copper coinage of Scotland. The farthings were issued about 1466 in the reign of James III (1460–88). The coins were of poor quality and were easy to counterfeit.

Two types of the farthings are known. The first showed on the obverse a large crown and the legend I REX SCOTORVM, on the reverse a saltire cross with two smaller saltire crosses in the side angles and VILLA EDINBVRG. The second type had on the obverse IR below five fleurs-de-lis in the shape of a crown and the legend IACOBVS DEI GRATIA, on the reverse was a saltire cross with smaller ones in three of the angles and a crown in the top one surrounded by VILLA EDINBVRG.

BLACK MONEY This money was imported illegally into England and circulated with the normal currency. It included *lushburgs* from Luxemburg, *dodkins (doitkins)*, *pollards*, *crocards*, *suskins*, *turneys* and *galley halfpence*.

It was also a term for early Scottish copper coins of the fifteenth century as opposed to 'white money' which was silver or billon. See also BLACK FARTHING.

BLACKSMITHS MONEY This is the name given to the crudely struck silver half-crowns which are thought to have been issued by supporters of Charles I from Kilkenny in 1649. In design, they resembled the crowns and half-crowns issued by the king from the Tower Mint at the beginning of his reign, with the equestrian figure of the King on the obverse and the royal arms on the reverse.

BODLE This copper coin was minted for use in Scotland from 1642 to 1697. It was worth half a plack, or two Scottish pennies

4a. Bodle of Charles II (obverse), and ×2

4b. Bodle of Charles II (reverse), and ×2

or a sixth of an English penny. Before 1642, the term *turner*
(*q.v.*) was used for the Scottish twopence and for a time both
names were present until the reign of William II (William III of
England) when bodle was the only one employed. It is thought
that the name is derived from Bothwell, the Master of the Mint.

The obverse design of the bodle showed the sovereign's monogram crowned during the reigns of Charles I, Charles II and
William and Mary. The 1677–9 issues of Charles II, and those
of William II (III of England), had a sword and sceptre, crossed,
with a crown above. The reverses of all issues depicted a Scottish
thistle, surrounded by the legend NEMO ME IMPVNE LACES-
SET ("No one shall hurt me with impunity").

BONNET PIECE   This coin was a variety of the gold Scottish
ducat issued in 1539 and 1540 by James V in his last coinage. It
was so called because the obverse bore a profile portrait of the
king wearing a flat bonnet decorated with fleur-de-lis and pellets. The legend read IACOBVS 5 DEI GR. SCOTORVM and
the date. The reverse had a crowned Scottish shield superimposed on a cross fleury surrounded by the inscription HONOR

5. Bonnet Piece (obverse and reverse)

REGIS IVDICIVM DILIGIT ("The King's strength loveth judgment") from Psalm 99, v. 4.

Two-thirds and one-third bonnet pieces also were issued in 1540. They differed from the main denomination in that the reverse showed a crowned Scottish shield flanked by I 5, for James V.

The bonnet piece weighed 88¼ grains and circulated for 40s. (£2) in Scotland, but in England it was only worth 3s. 4d. (16½p.).

The coin is also unique in that it was the first piece in the British Isles to bear the date. England did not date her coins until 1548 on the shillings of Edward VI.

BRASS This metal has only been used for one modern British coin, the twelve-sided threepenny piece, and then it was mixed with nickel. The nickel-brass coin was struck from 1937 to 1967 and on the introduction of a decimal currency in 1971 it was phased out with the rest of the £.s.d. coins still in circulation.

BREECHES MONEY This was the popular term for the coinage of the Commonwealth of 1649–60. It consisted of gold unites, double-crowns and crowns and silver crowns, half-crowns, shillings, sixpences, twopences, pennies and halfpennies. The central design on the reverse of all these rather plain coins consisted of two shields joined at the top and containing the cross of St George on the left and the Irish harp on the right. The

6. Commonwealth Crown (obverse and reverse)

shape made them resemble a pair of breeches of the time, and the coinage's nickname, which has since stuck, gave rise to Lord Lucas's remark to Charles II after the Restoration of 1660 that it was "a fit name for the coins of the Rump Parliament", *i.e.*, what was left of the Parliament that had been elected in 1640.

The obverse of each coin had only a shield with the cross of St George. The unique English legends on the higher denominations – THE COMMONWEALTH OF ENGLAND on the obverse and GOD WITH US on the reverse – also gave rise to another saying of the period by royalist supporters. They maintained that God was on one side and the Commonwealth on the other.

BRITAIN CROWN   James I of England issued this gold equivalent of the quarter-sovereign (25p.) in his second coinage in 1604. The design was similar to that on the double crown and had the same reverse legend HENRICVS ROSAS REGNA IACOBVS. Like the other coins of the period the value of the Britain crown was raised to 5s. 6d. (27½p.) in 1611 and when it returned to its old rate in 1619 the weight was reduced from 38¾ grains to 35. It was not minted again after 1660 and for its final issue Charles II had its weight decreased by another 2 grains.

As James VI of Scotland, James I, and later his son Charles I, struck Britain crowns and half-crowns for their northern kingdom. Like their English counterparts, these coins resembled the larger denomination of the double crown.

BRITANNIA   Britannia, the symbol of Britain, has appeared regularly on British coinage ever since the reign of Charles II, and the introduction of halfpennies and farthings in 1672. The

7a. Halfpenny of 1673 (reverse)

design, by John Roettier, Chief Engraver at the Mint, showed a seated Britannia in long, flowing robes, facing left, with a shield depicting the combined crosses of St George and St Andrew, and holding a spray of leaves in a raised right hand and a spear in her left. The model for the design is believed to have been Mrs Frances Stewart, Duchess of Richmond, a favourite of the king.

Although the Duchess may have been the model, the original idea for Britannia was taken from the copper coins of Hadrian (A.D.117–138) and Antoninus Pius (A.D. 138–161) during the Roman occupation of Britain. On these pieces Britannia appeared as a sad, despondent figure seated on a rock holding a spear, shield and standard. Later she was seen on a *sestertius* of Commodus (A.D. 177–192) but after that Britannia was neglected for nearly fifteen hundred years.

Except for slight modifications by other engravers, Roettier's design remained the same until 1797 when Küchler's interpretation of Britannia holding a trident and an olive branch, with the sea and a ship in the background, appeared on the 'Cartwheel' copper issue. Küchler referred to Britain's increasing maritime power.

A similar portrait of Britannia was depicted on the Bank of England dollar of 1804 (*q.v.*), the first appearance on a silver coin. This time, however, the spear replaced the trident. The symbol of interest, the beehive, was used instead of the ship, and a horn of plenty was put beneath the shield.

In 1821 the engraver introduced changes in the Britannia design which have remained to the present day. She wore a helmet for the first time and faced the right and the shield beside her showed the complete Union Jack. On the next design by William Wyon the olive branch was discarded.

Britannia appeared on the fractional half and third farthings of George IV and William IV. The tradition was continued on Victoria's third farthings until the change from copper to bronze took place. In this period Britannia made her second appearance on a silver coin, the Britannia groat, from 1836 to 1888.

When bronze replaced copper as the medium for small change coins in 1860, the sea motif with a lighthouse behind Britannia and a ship sailing out to sea returned. Leonard C. Wyon was the engraver of this new interpretation. For the Victorian 'veiled head' issue (1895–1901) both the ship and the lighthouse were omitted, the latter, however, made a return on the pennies of

7b. Florin of 1904 (reverse)

George VI and Elizabeth II. In both these reigns Britannia was dropped on the halfpenny and farthing in favour of Drake's *Golden Hind* and the wren, respectively.

On the silver British trade dollars issued for Asian colonies from 1895 to 1935, G.W. de Saulles, the Chief Engraver at the Mint showed a standing Britannia looking out to sea, holding a trident in her right hand, her left resting on her shield. The silver florin of Edward VII, by the same engraver, was similar in that Britannia was standing, but this time in the prow of a ship and with her robes flowing in the wind. The effect was all the more impressive. The model for this Britannia was Lady Susan Hicks-Beach, the daughter of the Master of the Mint.

With the coming of decimalization it was thought that Britannia would vanish completely, but it was decided to place her on the new fifty-penny piece. In Christopher Ironside's design, the sea and the lighthouse were omitted and the outstretched hand with the olive branch returned, as did the crouching lion, which had only previously appeared on the 1821–6 issue of the farthing.

BRITANNIA GROAT The groat re-appeared as a current British coin in 1836 in the reign of William IV. It was issued at the suggestion of Joseph Hume, a politician of the era, and it was from him that the coin took the nickname 'joey' which was used by the London cabbies, for he urged its use in payment of fares instead of the sixpence. The term *Britannia groat* came from the fact that the reverse depicted a seated Britannia similar to that on the copper coinage. These coins were struck nearly every year until 1855 when they were discontinued. There was, however, an extra issue in 1888, the second year of the Victorian jubilee coinage, for circulation in British Guiana.

8. Britannia Groat (reverse), and × 2½

All Britannia groats had milled edges and were a little smaller than the Maundy fourpences. The years 1838, 1840 and 1854 are common dates.

BRITT. This abbreviation of *Britanniarum*, meaning Great Britain and her possessions, was first used on Victorian coins, although the full form or *Britanniar* had appeared on coins since the recoinage of 1816. After the Boer War OMN. (meaning *all*) was added in 1902. This was intended as an expression of thanks to the colonies for their help in the conflict. On the coins of George VI BRITT. was abbreviated to BR. When the Commonwealth was inaugurated in 1954, the legend was discontinued.

BROAD The name *broad* is an alternative for the gold unite (*q.v.*) of the Stuart kings and the Commonwealth as well as being the main term for the twenty-shilling (£1) piece of Oliver Cromwell. Whereas the unite alluded to the union of the English and Scottish monarchies, the broad referred to the size of the coin.

In the reign of Charles II, the name was very often used for the hammered twenty-shilling piece as opposed to the milled guineas which originally circulated at the same value.

BRONZE In 1860 bronze replaced copper as the metal used in the production of the low value coins. Bronze is a copper alloy with a small percentage of tin and zinc, making the metal far more durable. This meant that the coins could remain in circulation longer before they had to be replaced. The bronze coins were smaller and thinner than the copper issues and therefore had the double advantage of being more convenient to carry as well as costing less to produce. Forty-eight bronze pennies could be minted from a pound of metal whereas only twenty-four could be made from the same amount of copper.

Bronze issues included the penny, halfpenny, farthing and third-farthing. The farthings of 1897 to 1917 were blackened to prevent confusion with half-sovereigns. Bronze is also used in the production of the three smallest decimal denominations: two new pence, one new penny and a new halfpenny.

BRVN.ET L. DVX S.R.I.A.TH. ET EL. This abbreviation for BRVNSVICENSIS ET LVNEBVRGENSIS DVX, SACRI ROMANI IMPERII ARCHITHESAVRARIVS ET ELECTOR, meaning "Duke of Brunswick and Lüneburg, High Treasurer and Elector of the Holy Roman Empire" appeared on British coins from 1714 to 1816, and referred to the German titles of the monarchs George I, George II, and George III. On the first coin of George I, the guinea of 1714, LVN was used instead of L. and the final part was PR. EL. (*Princeps Elector*, Prince Elector). On the pieces of George II and George III, the inscription appeared in an even shorter form, namely B. ET L. D. S.R.I.A.T. ET E.

BULL HEAD Half-crowns of George III issued in 1816 and 1817 were given the name 'bull head' issues because Benedetto Pistrucci's portrait showed the King with rather coarse, unflattering features, though apparently very life-like. The head was

9. 'Bull Head' Half-crown of George III (obverse)

seen from behind the shoulder and seemed to resemble a bull rather than a human. Later half-crowns were engraved with a smaller and more flattering bust of the King.

BUNGTOWN   This was a copper forgery of George II half-pennies of the 1770s and was minted in England. However, to prevent being accused of counterfeiting, the coiners used legends such as GEORGE RULES or DELECTANS RUS, thereby having the excuse that they were not making a true copy as the inscription had been changed intentionally. The majority of these coins were transported to the British colonies in America for circulation there.

BUN HEAD   The bronze issues from 1860 to 1894 showed Leonard Wyon's portrait of Queen Victoria with wreathed hair coiled in a bun at the back of the head. This hair-style resembled the one on the copper coins prior to 1860 and on silver and gold issues from 1837 to 1887, but the term 'bun head' referred only to the bronze coinage, particularly the penny.

C

CAROLUS   Another name for the unite of Charles I (*q.v.*).

CARTWHEEL   The huge, unwieldy penny and twopenny pieces which were issued in 1797 were familiarly known as 'cartwheels'. The twopence was over one and a half inches in diameter, and contained two ounces of copper, the coin's intrinsic metal value. The penny weighed half as much. Proofs of halfpenny and farthing cartwheels were struck but these denominations were never issued.

The manufacturers of these coins were Matthew Boulton and James Watt of the Soho Mint, Birmingham. Boulton's ideas on coinage were that coin blanks should be struck in a retaining collar, thus maintaining a constant diameter, that all coins should have an incuse legend which would be difficult to forge, and that each coin should contain its intrinsic metal value.

As the Royal Mint did not like to admit that its machines and techniques were out of date, Boulton had to wait nine years before he was given his first contract which requested from him 480 tons of pennies and 20 tons of twopences. The contract was completed on 9th June 1797.

10.   Cartwheel Twopence (obverse and reverse)

Cartwheels were minted for two years but all bore the same date, 1797. The obverse showed the legend GEORGIUS III D.G. REX and the bust of the king with the letter *K* for Küchler, who was also the designer of later coins for George III. The word *SOHO* was visible on the rocks below the seated figure of Britannia and her shield on the reverse. The inscription here read BRITANNIA 1797.

Cartwheels were discontinued because of Boulton's insistence on the coin containing its full metal value, for, as the price of copper rose, it was profitable for unscrupulous people to melt the coins and re-sell the metal.

CHANNEL ISLANDS   See JERSEY and GUERNSEY.

CHURCHILL CROWN   The reverse of the 1965 crown bore the name CHURCHILL and the bust of Sir Winston Churchill in his famous 'siren' suit which was adapted from a sculpture by Oscar Nemon. Apart from being the last crown to be issued under the £.s.d. system, the Churchill commemorative was noteworthy for having the largest mintage of any British crown up to that time since records were kept in 1816 and also for being the first piece to show the portrait of a commoner since the Oliver Cromwell pattern pieces of 1656 and 1658, provided that the figures of Britannia and St George are discounted.

COLONIAL COINS   See HALF-FARTHING, THIRD-FARTHING, QUARTER-FARTHING and THREEHALFPENCE.

COPPER   During the reign of James I, private shopkeepers circulated illegal issues of lead and pewter halfpenny and farthing tokens because there was a great shortage of small change. In 1613, to put a stop to this practice, the king authorized a certain Lord Harrington to strike copper farthings. These Harrington farthings (*q.v.*) were England's first copper coins, though Scotland had struck pieces in this metal as early as 1466, and Ireland had done so in the reign of Edward IV (1461–83). Patterns of pennies, halfpennies and farthings had been made in copper in 1601 for Elizabeth I, but an issue of coins was never struck.

The English monarchs considered it degrading to lend their portraits to base metal coins, but as silver fractions of a penny would have been too small to be practicable, licence was granted to a private individual. It was Charles II who issued the first regal copper coinage in 1672, patterns for which had been made in 1664. Halfpennies and farthings were then minted during most of the reigns after that but George III was the first to issue a copper penny – the famous cartwheel of 1797 (*q.v.*).

Copper was replaced by the more durable bronze for low value coins in 1860. It was used in the production of twopences, pennies, halfpennies, farthings, and half-, third- and quarter-farthings. Copper coins were demonetized on 1st January 1870.

COPPER NOSE This name was given to the latter silver issues of Henry VIII, because the base metal content of the coins was so high that parts of them were different in colour from the rest.

CROCARD This was one of the many types of thirteenth-century continental coins which circulated in England in the reign of Edward I. Two crocards, pollards or rosaries equalled one penny. They were, in fact, Flemish imitations of English pennies, being identical in their English counterpart except for the fact that the king was uncrowned. All three names are derived from devices on the coins themselves: *poll*, a head; *crocket*, a curl; and *rosary* from the rosette on the reverse.

CROOKSTON DOLLAR The Crookston or Cruickston dollar is the popular name given to the silver ryal of Mary Queen of Scots, during her marriage to Henry Darnley. It appeared together with two-third and one-third ryal pieces from 1565 to 1567 and replaced an earlier piece of 1565 which was withdrawn

11. Crookston Dollar (reverse)

because the consort's name appeared before the queen's in the legend.

On the completely new design, the obverse had MARIA ET HENRIC. DEI GRA. R. & R. SCOTORV. surrounding a crowned Scottish shield with a thistle on each side. The reverse showed a tortoise climbing a yew tree and it was from this motif that the coin received its name, for the tree was considered to represent the yew tree at Crookston, a residence of Lord Darnley, near Glasgow. The inscription DAT GLORIA VIRES ("Glory gives strength") on a scroll together with the date completed the reverse design and the legend read EXVRGAT DEVS ET DISSIPENTVR INIMICI EIVS ("Let God arise and let His enemies be scattered") from Psalm 68, v. 1.

CROWN England's first crown was a gold coin struck by Henry VIII in 1526 to compete with the French *écu au soleil*, and was valued at 4s. 6d. (22½p.). This 'crown of the rose' (*q.v.*), as it was called, was not a success and was soon replaced by the crown of the double rose (*q.v.*) rated at 5s. (25p.), a value which the crown has retained to this day except for a period of eight years from 1611 to 1619 when the Britain crown (*q.v.*) was worth 5s. 6d. (27½p.). The introduction of the crown marked the first debasement of fineness of English gold coinage and gave origin to the term *crown gold* (*q.v.*). The name *crown* had nothing to do with head covering of the monarch but was derived from the French *écu à la couronne*, of which it was a copy.

Gold crowns were issued in all reigns except those of Mary, and Philip and Mary, until the disappearance of hammered coinage in 1662. Up to the reign of Charles I, the obverses of most crowns (as opposed to the crown of the rose and crown of the double rose) showed a crowned portrait of the sovereign, and the reverses a crowned shield. The last gold crown, that of Charles II, showed the king with a laurel wreath around his head. The Commonwealth issues displayed a shield of the cross of St George on the obverse, and the same, together with an Irish harp, on the reverse.

The weight of the crown was originally 48 grains and for the most part it was gradually reduced by the Tudors until it was only 43 grains. As the Britain crown (*q.v.*) its weight was reduced even more.

As a counterpart to the German *thaler*, the first silver crown appeared in 1551 in the reign of Edward VI, in his coinage in which he attempted to restore silver to its former fineness. The obverse showed the boy-king mounted on a horse and the reverse showed a shield and a cross surrounded by the legend POSVI DEVM ADIVTOREM MEVM ("I have made God my helper"). The first crown also had the distinction of being the first English coin to display the date in Roman numerals. These pieces bore the mint mark Y, indicating that they were struck at Southwark by Sir John Yorke, and also a tun, the mark of Throgmorton of the Tower Mint.

12a. Crown of 1551 (obverse and reverse)

The first silver crown weighed 480 grains and was 11 ounces fine. Elizabeth I, the next monarch to issue silver crowns, increased the fineness by 2 pennyweights and reduced the weight to $464\frac{1}{2}$ grains, ratios which were retained until the recoinage of 1816. On the Elizabethan crowns, which did not appear until the end of the queen's reign in 1601 and 1602, the equestrian figure was replaced by a profile portrait facing left. However, James I and Charles I reverted to the original obverse design.

The Commonwealth crown was simple and plain in design, one side showing the shield of St George within a wreath and around that the English legend THE COMMONWEALTH OF ENGLAND, and the reverse showing the conjoined shield of England and Ireland within the inscription GOD WITH US.

The first milled crown in silver was the one which was issued as a pattern for Oliver Cromwell in 1658, Thomas Simon, more famous for his Petition crown (*q.v.*) five years later, engraved the bust of the Protector on the obverse and the shield on the reverse. To prevent clipping, the legend HAS NISI PERITVRVS MIHI ADIMAT NEMO (Let no one remove these [letters] under penalty of death) was added to the edge. On crowns issued after the restoration of the monarchy, this edge inscription was changed to DECVS ET TVTAMEN (An ornament and a safeguard) followed by the regnal year. From 1662 to 1751 all milled crowns were struck with almost the same design, a portrait of the sovereign on the obverse and the royal arms in four cruciform crowned shields on the reverse. After 1751 no more coins of this denomination were issued until 1818 because of the lack of silver.

With the great recoinage of 1816, the weight of the crown was to be reduced to 436 grains, but at least the fineness remained unaltered. The five-shilling piece did not, however, appear until two years later and was struck each year until 1822. The design which was similar for George III (1818, 1819, 1820) and George IV (1821, 1822) was the masterpiece of the talented Italian engraver, Benedetto Pistrucci. The obverses showed realistic busts of the two kings and the reverses the St George and the Dragon motif (*q.v.*). After 1822 it was considered that no more crowns were needed, although only a small number had been produced in the five years. Proofs, however, were issued in 1826 and 1831, for George IV and William IV.

In contrast to the dullness of the first Victorian crown of 1844, which showed the crowned royal arms within a wreath on the reverse, William Wyon produced a design to rival Pistrucci's St George and the Dragon. This was the famous Gothic crown of 1847 and the small number of 1853 proofs with the embroidered bodice on the queen's portrait, the cruciform shields and the medieval lettering. The jubilee and 'veiled head' issues returned to Pistrucci's design and the same was used for the small issue in the year of Edward VII's coronation.

The silver crown disappeared until 1927 when a small number was issued with a new design of a crown within a wreath. Limited numbers of the same type were struck each year until 1934. In addition, the silver content was reduced by almost half, as with all silver coins after 1920.

To mark the Silver Jubilee of George V in 1935, the crown became a commemorative piece, the role it played until the final issue in 1965. Examples of this are: the coronation crowns of

George VI and Elizabeth II in 1937 and 1953 (the former being the last to contain silver before the change to cupro-nickel), the 1951 crown for the Festival of Britain and the quater-centenary of the denomination, the 1960 crown for the British Exhibition in New York and the 1965 crown issued on the death of Sir Winston Churchill. It is also interesting to note that one of the last crowns, the 1953 coronation piece, reverted to the original design of the monarch on horseback.

12b. Churchill Crown (reverse)

The crown-size coin in Britain's decimal currency is the twenty-five new pence (*q.v.*).

CROWN GOLD   The crown of the rose (*q.v.*) was the first English coin to contain less than the standard fineness of 23 carats $3\frac{1}{2}$ grains, half a grain less than pure gold of 24 carats. The crown of the double rose (*q.v.*), issued later in the same year, was further debased from 23 to 22 carats. It is this alloy of 22 carats that is referred to as crown gold, as opposed to standard gold of 23 carats $3\frac{1}{2}$ grains fine.

CROWN OF THE DOUBLE ROSE   This coin superseded the crown of the rose and appeared in 1526, only a few months after the first unsuccessful issue of its forerunner. It was valued at 5s. (25p.) and weighed $57\frac{1}{2}$ grains. Its weight was greater than that of the crown of the rose but its fineness had been reduced to 22 carat crown gold (*q.v.*).

The crown of the double rose had the royal arms crowned on one side and a large double Tudor rose, also crowned, on the other. On both sides of the coin appeared the initials of Henry

VIII, alone, or with one of his consorts, Catherine of Aragon, Anne Boleyn or Jane Seymour. There are therefore a number of types of this coin, which was quite short-lived, for it did not appear again after 1544. The legend naturally included the king's titles and also the inscription RVTILANS ROSA SINE SPINA ("A dazzling rose without a thorn").

13. Crown of the Double Rose (obverse)

A half-crown of the double rose was also issued and it resembled the crown in design.

CROWN OF THE ROSE   This was the name of the first English crown which was struck in gold in 1526, in the second coinage of Henry VIII. It was an imitation of the French *couronne au soleil* and was introduced to compete with the same French coin that was circulating in Britain. However, to pass as the equivalent of the French coin at a value of 4s. 6d. (22½p.), the fineness in gold was reduced for the first time to 23 carats and the weight was fixed at about 51 grains.

14. Crown of the Rose (reverse)

The obverse of the coin showed a crowned shield of the royal arms and the legend HENRIC. 8 DEI GRA. REX AGL. Z FRANC., and the reverse showed HENRIC. RVTILANS ROSA SINE SPINA (A dazzling rose without thorns) surrounding a

Tudor rose superimposed on a cross with lions and crowned *H*s in the angles.

The crown of the rose is a great rarity and was replaced by the crown of the double rose (*q.v.*) in the same year. It could not have been a successful competitor to the French *écu* and its awkward monetary value would not have made it popular among the people.

CUMBERLAND JACKS Since Salic law prevented a woman from succeeding to the throne, Victoria could not assume the Hanoverian titles of her uncle, William IV, upon his death in 1837. Therefore the titles passed to the next male heir, one of her other uncles, Ernest Augustus, Duke of Cumberland. The duke was an unpopular man in England. First of all, his personal appearance left something to be desired. Stories said that he had received scars after an attack from his Corsican valet, whom he was thought to have murdered later and he was said to have committed other crimes in addition to this. Moreover, he was opposed to the reform of Parliament, the emancipation of the Roman Catholics, and other liberal measures. He also wished to become King of Great Britain.

To express pleasure at his departure, TO HANOVER tokens, in brass, were minted as a satirical gesture as well as for use as card counters. The obverse usually depicted the new queen and the legend VICTORIA REGINA and sometimes the date below.

15. Cumberland Jack (reverse)

The reverses showed a picture of the crowned duke on horseback, with a dragon below. In some versions he had a monkey's face. The reverse legend was mostly TO HANOVER with the date below if it had not already appeared on the obverse. The commonest date was 1837.

It is thought that some of these 'Cumberland jacks' may have been passed as sovereigns or half-sovereigns of the period when the brass was newly minted.

CUPRO-NICKEL In order to repay the United States the large amounts of silver borrowed during the Second World War, the British Government decided to withdraw all the silver coinage in circulation and replace it with a base metal currency made of cupro-nickel, an alloy of 75 per cent copper and 25 per cent nickel. The first coins were struck in 1947 and in appearance differed only slightly from the silver issues; the milling on the edge, however, was closer. The only coins not to be struck in the new metal were the Maundy denominations, the standard of which was restored to .925 standard silver.

D

DANDIPRAT In Tudor times this term was used to describe any small coin. It is often considered that people referred to the half-groat or twopence with this name.

DANEGELD This refers to the tax levied by Aethelred II ('The Unready') on his English subjects in order to raise money to buy off the Danish invaders. Payments were made to the Danes in pennies, which the king struck in large quantities, and many of these have been found in hoards in Scandinavia.

DATES The first English coin to bear a date was the silver shilling of 1548. This date was written in Roman numerals, but later Arabic figures were used. The coins of Elizabeth I frequently bore the year, but dating did not become standard practice until 1662. Otherwise, a coin could only be dated by examining the mint mark or alternative distinguishing characteristics.

The year 1967 was the final date to be used on £.s.d. coins, with the exception of those struck in gold, Maundy pieces and the special proof set dated 1970, which was issued by the Royal Mint for collectors. It is interesting to note that the sixpence of George V, struck from 1927 to 1936, included the letters A.D. on both sides of the date.

Cupro-nickel decimal coins date from 1968 (5p. and 10p.) and 1969 (50p.), and the bronze 2p., 1p., and ½p. from 1971.

The Scots began to date their coins earlier than the English. The first example was the bonnet-piece of James V which was dated 1539.

DECIMAL COINS The first attempt to introduce a type of decimal coinage in Britain can be said to have taken place in the reign of Charles II when Sir Charles Petty proposed that a penny should be split into five farthings, thereby making a pound (£1) equal to 1,200 farthings, instead of 960. Later Queen Anne supported this idea. About the same time Sir Christopher Wren suggested that an ounce of silver should have one hundred divisions.

The first real attempt at decimalization, however, was made soon after Queen Victoria's accession to the throne. Sir John Bowring finally withdrew his proposal in Parliament that a pound be divided into hundredths, on condition that a tenth-of-a-pound piece be issued to test the public's reaction. At the same time many patterns of decimal coins were struck. In 1848 the Mint ceased striking half-crowns and issued the florin, a tenth of a pound (*q.v.*). However, the idea was abandoned, and in the early 1870s the half-crown was struck again in large quantities, side by side with the florin.

The next step was made in December 1961, when Parliament set up a Committee of Inquiry under the Earl of Halsbury to investigate the potential practicability of a decimal currency. In 1966 it was decided to implement the findings of the report first published in 1963. The Decimal Currency Act came into force in 1967, and a Decimal Currency Board to advise the Government and the public was formed in the same year.

The florin became the link between £.s.d. and decimalization. Decimal coins were introduced gradually, first the ten and five new pence, the equivalents of the florin and shilling respectively. Towards the end of 1969 the fifty new pence was circulated and the ten-shilling note was withdrawn. During the change-over period the half-crown and the halfpenny also ceased to be legal tender. The rest of the decimal coins (2p., 1p., and ½p.) appeared on 15th February 1971, and after that date the rest of the £.s.d. coins (6d., 3d., and 1d.) were to be phased out.

However, after due consideration the 6d. was not demonetized for, at the time, it was a very popular coin in slot machines. Inflation, the public's adaptation to the new coinage, and the awkward amount it represented in decimal currency (2½p.) meant that the sixpence was not often used in everyday transactions although it remained legal tender until 1980.

To introduce the new decimal coins and acquaint the public with them, the Royal Mint produced five million sets of 10p., 5p., 2p., 1p., and ½p. coins in plastic wallets in 1968, and these were sold through the banks. In 1972 the first twenty-five new pence coin was issued to commemorate the silver wedding of Queen Elizabeth II and the Duke of Edinburgh and this was the equivalent of the crown in the £.s.d. system.

See also individual denominations.

DECLARATION TYPE   Various coins of Charles I, struck at provincial mints, contained the king's declaration to the people on the reverse, instead of the royal shield. The declaration ran RELIG. PROT. LEG. ANG. LIBER. PAR. in two or three lines and meant "The Protestant religion, the laws of England and the liberties of Parliament."

See also OXFORD CROWN.

DECVS ET TVTAMEN   This Latin quotation, meaning "an ornament and a safeguard", was first engraved round the edge of the five guinea and crown pieces in the reign of Charles II. It appeared regularly on crowns until 1935, but was not used again until the introduction of the pound coin in 1983. The inscription was originally in place of a milled edge and prevented the clipping of silver from the coins by unscrupulous members of the public.

DEI GRATIA   William I first used this inscription on his seals. It is the Latin for "by the grace of God". It first appeared on coins on the Edward I groat of 1279, and has been part of the legend on British coins ever since, except for the so-called 'godless florin' of 1849 (*q.v.*).

The inscription also appears as D.G., DEI GRA., DI. GRA.

DEMY   James I (1406–37) and James II (1437–60) of Scotland issued a gold demy which weighed 54 grains and had a value of 9s. (45p). The obverse showed the Scottish lion in a lozenge-shaped shield, the reverse a saltire cross with a fleur-de-lis in each of the side angles, within a tressure of six arcs, the points of

16a. Demy of James I (obverse), and ×2

16b. Demy of James I (reverse), and ×2

which were headed by a fleur-de-lis. The reverse legend read
SALVVM FAC POPVLVM TVVM DOMINE ("O Lord, save
Thy people") from Psalm 28, v. 9.

James I also struck a half-demy with a similar design.

DEMY-LION   This was a Scottish gold coin first struck by
Robert III (1390–1406) and was valued at 2s. 6d. (12½p.). Later
in Robert's reign, the weight of the coin, like that of the lion, was
reduced by a third to 20 grains. James II (1437–60) was the next
monarch to issue the demy-lion, which was now referred to as a
half-lion, and he doubled its value to 5s. (25p.), but only increased its weight by 7 grains. James IV (1488–1513) was the
only other monarch to strike the half-lion which, in his reign, circulated at 6s. 8d. (33½p.), with a slight decrease in weight from
the previous issue.

The design of the first demy-lions showed the Scottish shield
on the obverse, and a saltire cross with fleurs-de-lis and trefoils in
the angles on the reverse. The demy-lions of James II and James
IV copied the design on the lion with the Scottish shield on the
obverse and the figure of St Andrew, crucified on a saltire cross,
on the reverse.

DENARIUS   This is the Latin word for a denier (*q.v.*).

DENIER   A denier was a 240th part of a *livra* (*q.v.*). The
Anglo-Gallic penny struck by Henry II for Aquitaine was also
called a denier. See also ANGLO-GALLIC COINS.

DESIGNERS   See ENGRAVERS and INITIALS.

DINAR   King Offa of Mercia (757–796) famous for his series of silver pennies, struck a unique gold dinar which was a copy of an Arabian gold piece of the same name, with the king's title added to the legend.

DNS.HIB.   See HIB.

DODKIN   This is the diminutive of doit (*q.v.*).

DOIT   The doit, the English form of the Dutch *duit* was the name for the *eighth of stuiver* which circulated in the Netherlands. The name is said to have come from the French *d'huit* (eighth part). These same coins were also circulated in England and Scotland until they were prohibited in the seventeenth century. They, and other inferior coins, were brought to the British Isles by foreign traders.

DOLLAR   In the late eighteenth century there was an acute shortage of silver, due to the expansion of Britain's commerce and industry. In addition, as silver bullion on the open market at the time cost 5s. $6\frac{1}{2}$d. (28p.) an ounce, which could only be used to mint 5s. 2d. (26p.) of coins, it was most uneconomical for the Royal Mint to undertake the striking of a new issue of small silver pieces. In 1797, therefore, the Bank of England circulated Spanish-American eight-real pieces struck at mints in Central and South America. As the Spanish dollar was slightly lighter than the British crown, its value was fixed at 4s. 9d. (24p.), instead of 5s. (25p.). The Bank of England still made a profit of 5d. (2p.) on each coin and, not being worth as much as their current value, the dollars were counterfeited.

17a. Dollar of George III (obverse) with oval countermark, and detail ×4

Most reals have the head of Charles III or Charles IV of Spain, countermarked with an oval stamp of the head of George III, which was used for ordinary hallmarking of silver. This gave rise to the saying "The Bank of England to make its dollars pass, stamped the head of a fool on the neck of an ass", and as the coins were only worth 24p., another popular comment was "two kings' heads not worth a crown". A half-dollar was also issued with this oval stamp.

In 1799, to check the widespread counterfeiting, an octagonal puncheon for Maundy coins was used to make a countermark with a larger bust on the coins.

In 1800 the rise in the cost of silver meant that the dollars had to be revalued to 5s. (25p.). Four years later Matthew Boulton of Birmingham received the contract to restrike the whole coin with a new design engraved by Conrad Küchler, who had produced the art work for the Cartwheel penny of 1797 (*q.v.*). The obverse of the new coin showed the laureate draped bust of George III, and on the reverse Britannia, making her first appearance on a silver coin, is seated within an oval ring bearing the inscription FIVE SHILLINGS DOLLAR. The Bank of England, by having its name on the reverse as well, wanted to show that the coins were not a regal issue. These overstruck pieces were produced in 1804, 1810 and 1811, but all bore the original date.

17b. Bank of England Dollar (obverse and reverse)

In his second Scottish coinage, from 1675 to 1682, Charles II issued a silver dollar of 429 grains to replace the four merks of the previous issue. The fractions of half-, quarter-, eighth- and sixteenth-dollar were also minted. The obverses showed the laureate bust of the king; the reverses of the four highest denominations depicted the four quarters of the royal arms in cruciform, with thistles in the angles and interlinked *C*'s in the centre, whilst the sixteenth of a dollar had the cross of St Andrew with a crown in the centre, and the emblems thistle, rose, harp and fleur-de-lis in the angles.

See also TRADE DOLLAR.

DORRIEN AND MAGENS SHILLING   In 1798, the firm of Dorrien and Magens sent silver bullion to the Mint to be made into shillings of the same design as the 1787 issue – a laureate cuirassed bust of George III on the obverse and four cruciform shields of the royal arms, with crowns in the angles, on the reverse.

Since no order had been given for the coins to be struck, the shillings were confiscated and melted down. A few survived, however, and, being rare, command a high price from collectors.

DOUBLE CROWN   This term is used for the gold half-sovereign of the second coinage of James I. The double crown or half-unite was a smaller version of the unite, as the sovereign of this period was called (*q.v.*). The obverse showed a crowned bust of the king and the reverse a crowned plain shield of the royal arms, with I R (*Iacobvs Rex*) on each side. The reverse legend read HENRICVS ROSAS REGNA IACOBVS ("Henry united the roses, James the realms"). A similar piece was issued for Charles I and Charles II.

The same denomination was also struck by James I and Charles I for Scotland, where it was worth £6, Scottish currency being one twelfth of the value of English money. The first Scottish issue differed from the English in that the king wore a Scottish crown. Later issues also showed a Scottish shield on the reverse with the Scottish arms in the first and fourth quarters.

DOUBLE FLORIN   This was a new silver denomination introduced in 1887 in the jubilee issue of Queen Victoria. It proved to be an unpopular coin as its size caused it to be confused with the silver crown, although the reverse designs were hardly alike, the latter displaying St George and the Dragon on the reverse, whilst the double florin showed four cruciform shields of the royal arms as depicted on the two-shilling piece. In diameter, however, the double florin measured 36mm., only $2\frac{3}{4}$mm. less than the crown. The coin was nicknamed the 'barmaid's nightmare', because the employees in the public houses easily mistook the coin for a crown when serving their customers in the poor light.

The double florin was discontinued in 1890. There are two varieties of the 1887 type. The figure 1 in the date appears as a Roman numeral (I), the other as an Arabic 1. Neither type is particularly scarce.

Other patterns were made to re-introduce the denomination in 1890, 1911 and 1950. The George V pattern of 1911, designed by Huth, showed a bare-headed draped bust of the king facing left, with the inscription GEORGIVS V DEI GRATIA on one side, and on the other, BRITANNIARVM REX 1911, surrounding four crowned cruciform shields of England, Ireland, Scotland and Wales, with the three legs of Man superimposed on a star in the centre. The emblems of the four nations; rose, thistle, leek and shamrock, appeared in the angles. The 1950 pattern was much less ornate, showing the king, George VI, facing left, and the date on the obverse and St George in the Garter on the reverse.

DOUBLE GROAT The unusual denomination with the value of eightpence (8d. $= 3\frac{1}{2}$p.) was struck in silver for Ireland in the reign of Edward IV. It was introduced in 1467 at a time when silver bullion was in short supply. Therefore the double groat was struck at the same weight of the previous issue, 43 to 45 grains, and the value of the piece was doubled.

The coin showed a crowned facing bust of the king on the obverse, and a rose in the centre of a large radiant sun on the reverse. The same rose and sun design was featured on the smaller groat, half-groat and penny.

In 1470 a new heavy coinage was introduced and the double groat was devalued to fourpence.

DOUBLE LEOPARD See FLORIN.

DUBLIN HALFPENNY In the reign of Charles II (1660–85), at the same time as the issue of St Patrick's money (*q.v.*) in Ireland, a halfpenny appeared bearing the Irish harp, crowned, on the obverse, and the Dublin coat of arms surrounded by THE DUBLIN HALFPENNIE on the reverse. The exact origin of this coin still remains a mystery.

DUBLIN MONEY This term is used to refer to the silver crowns and half-crowns issued by the Marquis of Ormonde, the Viceroy of Ireland, in an attempt to proclaim Charles II King of Ireland after his father's execution in 1649. The obverse contained a large crown and the reverse the value in Roman numerals. The coins were quite light, the crown weighing about 330 grains as opposed to the $464\frac{1}{2}$ grains for regal issues.

Dublin money also refers to the third issue of Inchiquin money (*q.v.*), which consisted of crowns and half-crowns struck in Dublin.

DUCAT The original Scottish ducat was struck by James V but was called a bonnet piece (*q.v.*). In 1558, James's daughter, Mary Stuart, issued a heavier coin of 118 grains, named a ducat, which was valued at the higher rate of £3. This was during her marriage to Francis, the French Dauphin, and both appeared face to face on the obverse of the coin. The reverse showed a cross made up of eight interlinked dolphins with Lorraine crosses (‡) in the angles. The next and last ducat, that of James VI in 1580,

18. Ducat of James VI (obverse)

which, on the obverse, depicted the king wearing a ruff, weighed considerably less than his mother's coin but circulated at £4. Not only did it weigh fractionally more than 94 grains, but also the fineness of the gold had been reduced by 1 carat to 21 carats.

DUMP A small thick coin is called a dump, but the term is often used to describe the copper halfpennies of 1717 and 1718, and farthings of 1717 of George I, which were struck on quite a deep flan.

DUODECIMAL COINS   The duodecimal system of reckoning in units of twelve originated in ancient Rome and spread throughout Europe. A pound of silver was divided into 240 parts, one part being a *denarii* (*q.v.*). The pound was, therefore, a money of account, as was the *solidus* which came later and contained 12 *denarii*.

The Anglo-Saxons adopted the principle of 240 pence in one pound and later the Normans introduced the shilling as a money of account corresponding to the *solidus*. In time, pounds and shillings appeared as coins, with twelve pennies making one shilling and twenty shillings one pound. Great Britain, the Republic of Ireland and the Channel Islands retained a duodecimal coinage until 1971 when a currency based on the less cumbersome but not so versatile decimal system was introduced.

E

E. This letter, appearing under the effigy of Queen Anne, signifies that the coin was struck at the mint in Edinburgh. Edinburgh denominations included crowns, half-crowns, shillings and sixpences dated 1707, 1708 and 1709, the last year of the mint's operation.

Edinburgh was, of course, also the major mint of the Scottish monarchs and of the first Stuart kings of Great Britain.

EASTERLING, ESTERLING These were popular names given to the foreign imitations of the English penny which circulated in the twelfth, thirteenth and fourteenth centuries. The names also applied to small, silver coins of Europe at the time. Other terms were *crocard* and *pollard* (*q.v.*).

The traders from the Hanseatic towns on the Baltic were known by the same name.

ECCLESIASTICAL COINS These coins were struck by high ranking officials of the Catholic Church, at their own private mints, from the time of the Norman Conquest until the sixteenth century. The most notable and longest existing mints were those of the Archbishops of Canterbury and York and the Bishop of Durham.

After the break with Rome, the Act of Supremacy of 1535 made Henry VIII supreme Head of the Church of England. The King ordered the dissolution of the monasteries and the secularization of church lands. It was at this time that the ecclesiastical mints closed permanently.

ECU   See ABBEY CROWN.

EDINBURGH BUST The coins of Queen Anne with the Edinburgh mint mark under the portrait are referred to as the Edinburgh bust types. See also E.

EIC   These letters occasionally appeared under the portrait of
George II on gold coins from 1729 to 1739 to indicate that the
metal was supplied by the East India Company.

19. Guinea of 1729–32 (obverse) with EIC inscription

EIGHTEEN PENCE   In order to put a stop to the widespread
circulation of silver tokens, the Bank of England issued pieces of
this value from 1811 to 1816. The obverse of the first issue
showed a laureate bust of George III in armour, within the
legend GEORGIUS III DEI GRATIA REX, the second just a laureate head of the king surrounded by the same inscription. The
reverse of both issues had the words BANK TOKEN 1s. 6d.
and the date within a wreath. The coin had a plain edge.
    See also THREE-SHILLING PIECE.

EIGHT-OF-UNITE   Together with other unite denominations (*q.v.*), the gold eight-of-unite was issued by Charles I
for use in Scotland in 1637. The equivalent of a half-crown, it
was also called a Britain half-crown. Similar to other unite
denominations, the obverse had a crowned portrait of the
king, and the reverse had the royal arms crowned.

EIGHT-SHILLING PIECE   See SIXTEEN-SHILLING PIECE.

ELEPHANT, ELEPHANT & CASTLE   These two badges,
the former being used before 1674, appeared on gold and

20. Guinea of 1674–84 (obverse) with Elephant and Castle

silver coins from Charles II to George I. The second emblem is particularly rare on silver pieces. They donated the metal supplied by the Africa Company which operated in Guinea, later the Gold Coast and now Ghana.

EMERGENCY MONEY   Or 'Money of Necessity'. See under individual headings of Gun Money, Siege Pieces, Blacksmith's Money, Dublin Money, Inchiquin Money, Kilkenny Money, Ormonde Money.

From 1645 to 1647, the four southern Irish towns of Bandon, Kinsale, Youghal and Cork issued emergency money during the occupation by Parliamentary troops. The individual coins can be identified by the town's name or initial stamped on it. All four towns struck copper farthings. In addition, Youghal minted brass twopences and pewter threepences, while Cork's siege money also included silver shillings and sixpences and copper halfpennies.

Emergency money is a term for all unofficial coinages and therefore includes tokens, but it is usually applied in this country to the Civil War coinages and the gun money of James II.

ENAMELLED COINS   In the last quarter of the nineteenth century, the Birmingham jewellers W. H. Probert and Edwin Steele became famous in the art of enamelling coins which were then made into brooches or pendants. Since their success the art of enamelling coins has been imitated and continued.

Originally the long and tedious work entailed cutting out by hand $\frac{1}{16}$ in. from the design of the coin, which was usually silver, and filling it with a variety of colours of enamel paint. The modern method of enamelling coins makes use of machine processes.

ENGLISH SHILLING   The English shilling belonged to the final period of duodecimal coinage from 1937 to 1966, in the reigns of George VI and Elizabeth II, and was so called because the reverse design differed from that on the 'Scottish shilling' (*q.v.*). Like other silver coins of the time it was struck in an alloy containing 50 per cent silver until 1946, and thereafter in cupronickel.

The reverse design of the George VI shilling was similar to the one issued by his father and depicted a lion on an English crown.

In addition, two roses, the English national flower, broke the legend. The reverse of the Elizabeth II shilling showed the English quarter of the royal arms – three leopards passant guardant – crowned.

21. (*left to right*) English Shilling of George VI (reverse); English Shilling of Elizabeth II (reverse)

An extra English shilling dated 1970 appeared in the Royal Mint proof sets of £.s.d. currency struck in the same year.

See also SCOTTISH SHILLING.

ENGRAVERS   Throughout the centuries the Royal Mint has employed many notable engravers who have produced a large number of fine coins. The renaissance of coin portraiture began with the testoon of Henry VII, first struck in 1504. Alexander de Brugsal was responsible for the realistic profile portrait of the King. This was a departure from the full-face stereotyped busts characteristic of previous reigns.

In 1625 Nicholas Briot came from France to take up a post as an engraver at the Royal Mint under Charles I. The fine workmanship of Briot's coins was enhanced by the fact that they were struck on the machinery he introduced at the Mint to produce round symmetrical blanks. Another well-known engraver of the reign of Charles I was Thomas Rawlins, who designed the famous Oxford crown (*q.v.*) during the period of the Civil War, when the King's mint was established in that city.

Thomas Simon was Chief Engraver during the time of the Commonwealth and he engraved the patterns for the coinage of Oliver Cromwell. He is perhaps most famous for his Petition Crown (*q.v.*), with which he hoped to persuade Charles II to re-instate him as Chief Engraver above John Roettier. Roettier was a Dutchman who had become acquainted with the King during the latter's exile in Holland, and following the Restoration he had been offered a position in the Mint. Simon's petition did not succeed and Roettier designed the first coins to be produced on the new milling machinery installed in the Mint.

Thomas Croker was Chief Engraver from the reign of Queen Anne to that of George II. He was succeeded by John Tanner who also held his position under George III. From the time of the great recoinage in 1816 until late in the Victorian era, the most famous engravers were Benedetto Pistrucci and members of the Wyon family (*q.v.*)

See also INITIALS.

F

FARTHING   The farthing began as one of the four parts of a penny cut along the lines of the cross which was the central motif of the reverse design. The name of the coin comes from the Anglo-Saxon *feorthing* (fourthling or fourth part). The first round farthing, which was originally known by the Latin *ferlingus*, was issued by Edward I in 1279, although John had issued such a denomination for Ireland while he was Lord of that country at the beginning of the same century.

The design on Edward's farthing was the same as that on the penny and the weight was at first a little more than $6\frac{3}{4}$ grains, before falling to $5\frac{1}{2}$ grains in 1280. The early coins were unpopular and therefore uncommon because of their minute size. In addition, they suffered such a reduction in weight that by the time Edward VI came to the throne in 1547 they were only $2\frac{1}{2}$ grains, but later, "while reducing the fineness considerably", the young King increased the weight of the farthing to 3 grains.

Owing to the rising price of bullion, the farthing could not be struck in silver any longer, and the first copper issues appeared under licence in the reign of James I. (See HARRINGTON, LENNOX, RICHMOND, MALTRAVERS and ROSE FARTHINGS). The first regal issues did not appear until 1672. From 1684 to 1692 the farthing was struck in tin with a square plug of copper in the centre and the edge inscription NVMMORVM FAMVLVS ("Servant of coins"), in an attempt to prevent counterfeiting, but owing to the poor durability of this metal copper was preferred again from 1694 to 1860. In 1860 the farthing became a smaller and more

22. Farthing of 1953 (reverse)

manageable bronze coin. From 1897 to 1917 the bronze was blackened to prevent confusion with the similar sized half-sovereign. Until 1936 the farthing was a smaller version of the penny, but for the smallest piece in the coinage of George VI a new design was accepted – the wren, Britain's smallest bird. The last issue of the farthing was made in 1956 because its purchasing power had been reduced to almost nothing and it was demonetized on 1st January 1961.

F.D., FID. DEF. These abbreviations of the Latin phrase *fidei defensor*, meaning "defender of the faith", have been a permanent feature of the legend on British coins since the time of George I, with the single exception of the 'godless florin' (*q.v.*) of 1849. The title creates a false impression, for "the faith" refers to Catholicism and not the Church of England, of which the British sovereign is the temporal head, for it was conferred on Henry VIII by the Pope for his treatise against Luther. The King later renounced the Catholic faith when the Pope would not allow him to divorce his first wife, Catherine of Aragon, but he kept the title. The first inscription to appear on a coin was REGINA FIDEI on the quarter angel of Elizabeth I.

FERLINGUS This was the original name for a farthing (*q.v.*).

FIFTY NEW PENCE The shape of this coin, an equilateral curve heptagon, was a revolutionary new concept when it was introduced in October 1969 to replace the ten-shilling note. It was the third decimal piece to be circulated before the changeover to decimal currency. The obverse showed a portrait of Elizabeth II by Arnold Machin, the reverse saw the return of Britannia to a 'silver' coin, the first time since the groat of the last century. Christopher Ironside's design showed Britannia leaning against a shield displaying the Union Jack, holding a trident in her right hand and extending an olive branch in her left. A lion was seated beside her and the figure 50 appeared in the exergue. For 1973 a new design by David Wynne, consisting of nine joined hands in a circle, to mark Britain's entry into the European Community, replaced Britannia. Later issues reverted to the original design. The word 'NEW' was dropped in 1982.

See MAN for commemorative fifty-penny pieces.

FIFTY-SHILLING PIECE This gold pattern was the highest denomination bearing the portrait of Oliver Cromwell. It showed the protector's laureate bust facing left and the legend OLIVARD D.G.R.P. ANG. SCO. ET HIB. PRO. ("Oliver, by the Grace of God, Protector of the Republic of England, Scotland and Ireland") on the obverse. The reverse had a crowned shield with the cross of St George in the first and fourth quarters, the cross of St Andrew in the second, and the Irish harp in the third. Cromwell's own emblem, a lion rampant, appeared in an escutcheon of pretence. The legend read PAX QVAERITUR BELLO ("Peace is sought by war").

Like the broad and the silver coins, the fifty-shilling piece was designed by Thomas Simon and produced on Pierre Blondeau's minting machine in 1656.

FINEWORK COINS   This term describes the particularly well-engraved five, two and one guineas of 1701. The bust of King William III is far more ornate than the previous types.

FIVE-GUINEA PIECE   The five-guinea piece was struck regularly from the reign of Charles II to that of George II. Patterns were also issued in 1770, 1773, and 1777 in the reign of George III but none were struck for official circulation. The five-guinea piece was replaced by the five pounds after the recoinage of 1816.

See GUINEA.

FIVE NEW PENCE   Together with the ten new pence, this denomination was issued in 1968 as Britain's first decimal coin. It was interchangeable with the shilling, its equivalent in the £.s.d. system, while the latter gradually disappeared from circulation. The obverse showed Arnold Machin's portrait of Elizabeth II, and the reverse a Scottish thistle crowned with a figure 5 below, by Christopher Ironside. Like the shilling and the other 'silver' coins in the decimal coinage, the five new pence is minted in cupro-nickel. The word 'NEW' ceased to be used from 1982.

FIVEPENCE   The Bank of Ireland issued fivepenny tokens (2p.) in 1805 and 1806, in the same series as the six shillings and the ten and thirty pence (*q.v.*). These silver pieces showed a laureate draped bust of George III with GEORGIVS III DEI GRATIA on the obverse and on the reverse were five lines of writing, BANK/TOKEN/FIVE/PENCE/IRISH/, and the date.

FIVE-POUND PIECE   This gold coin of $607\frac{1}{4}$ grains and 22 carats fine was the direct descendant of the five-guinea piece after the recoinage of 1816. It was first struck as a pattern in 1820 and has occasionally been issued since, mainly as a proof and chiefly in coronation and jubilee years. The dates are 1820, 1826, 1839, 1887, 1893, 1902, 1911, 1937, 1953, 1980 and 1981. 1887, 1893 and 1902 were the only years when non-proof specimens were minted. All types are now very expensive, the 1820 pattern being the rarest of all. With two exceptions, the five pounds has shown the same design, the portrait of the monarch on the obverse and Pistrucci's St George and the Dragon on the reverse. However, the 1826 version showed a draped crowned shield on the reverse, whilst the 1839 version bore the motif of Una and the Lion (*q.v.*).

See also MAN.

FIVE-SHILLING PIECE   See TEN-SHILLING PIECE and SIXTY-SHILLING PIECE.

FLORIN   The name originated from the Italian city of Florence, which first struck the florin as a gold coin in 1252. Almost a century later, in 1344, Edward III authorized the issue of the first English gold florin which was worth six shillings (30p.) and was also called a 'double leopard'.

23. Florin of 1344 (obverse and reverse)

This issue of the florin and the two minor pieces, the leopard and the helm (*q.v.*), suffered the same fate as the gold penny of Henry III (*q.v.*), which was an English sovereign's first attempt since the Norman Conquest to establish a gold coinage. The florin and its fractions were discontinued in the same year. However, by this time it was proving necessary for England, as a trad-

ing nation, to have a gold coinage, and therefore 1344 also saw
the introduction of the noble (*q.v.*), which existed much longer
than its predecessor.

The gold florin weighed 108 grains and was 23 carats $3\frac{1}{2}$
grains fine. The obverse showed the legend, EDWR.D. GRA.
REX ANGL.Z FRANC. DNS. HIB., around the king holding a
sceptre and orb and seated on the throne beneath a Gothic
canopy with a fleur-de-lis background. A lion was depicted on
either side of the throne. The reverse had an elaborate cross with
a crown at the end of each limb, all within a quatrefoil. Four
English lions (passant grandant) took up positions in the span-
drels outside the quatrefoil. The reverse legend was taken from
Luke, Chapter 4, v. 30, and read IHC TRANSIENS PER
MEDIVM ILLORVM IBAT ("Jesus, passing through the midst
of them, went His way").

The florin did not re-appear until 1849 when it was struck as a
silver coin weighing 174 grains and valued at two shillings
(10p.), one tenth of a pound. This issue, the so-called 'godless
florin' (*q.v.*) and the subsequent Gothic florin (*q.v.*), marked the
first attempt on the part of the British Government to introduce
a decimal coinage. This piece was called a florin this time because it was similar in value to the Dutch and Austrian coin of
the same name, not because of its gold ancestor. At the same
time, issues of the half-crown were suspended but, as interest in a
decimal coinage lapsed, it re-appeared in 1875 and both it and
the florin circulated side by side. When the government finally
decided to introduce a decimal coinage in the 1960s, the florin
served as the main link between the old and the new currencies as
it was already a decimal fraction of a pound.

The florin was struck in silver (and part silver from 1920)
until 1947 when like the rest of the British silver coins (excluding
Maundy), it was minted in cupro-nickel. The silver and cupro-
nickel florin was a coin which always had a milled edge.

One of the finest modern coins was the florin of Edward VII,
which had a reverse of a standing Britannia in the prow of a ship.
However, this delicate design could not withstand the rough
treatment it received in everyday transactions and wore away
quickly (See also BRITANNIA). Consequently the florins of
George V reverted to the old motif of the royal arms in quatrefoil, as used on the jubilee coinage of Victoria. The florins of
George VI and Elizabeth II broke away from the tradition of pre-

vious monarchs and displayed, in different treatments, the floral emblems of England, Scotland and Ireland – the rose, thistle, and shamrock – rather than a variation of the royal coat of arms.

FORTY-FOUR-SHILLING PIECE This was a rare Scottish gold coin of $78\frac{1}{2}$ grains, issued in 1553 and 1557, in the reign of Mary. There were various types but basically they all had the same design of a crowned Scottish shield on the obverse and the Queen's crowned monogram within DILIGITE IVSTICAM ("Observe justice") and the date on the reverse. Its half, the twenty-two-shilling piece, was only struck in 1553 and was similar in design.

FORTY-PENNY PIECE The silver quarter merk or half noble of Charles I, which was issued for Scotland from 1636 to 1642, was called the forty-penny piece by virtue of the Roman numerals XL behind the King's portrait on the obverse. The legend SALVS REIP. SVPR. LEX ("The safety of the people is the supreme law") surrounded a crowned thistle on the reverse.

FORTY-SHILLING PIECE This large silver coin was first issued in 1582. The obverse showed the portrait of James VI of Scotland, crowned and armed, holding a sword in his right hand. The crowned shield on the reverse was between the initials I and R and the Roman numerals XL, and an S (shilling) signifying the value of the coin. The legend was HONOR REGIS IVDICIVM DILIGIT (The King's power loveth judgment).

Fractions were also minted. They were thirty-, twenty-, and ten-shilling pieces. They differed from the other coin in the Roman numerals on the reverse, *i.e.*, XXX, XX and X respectively.

See also SIXTY-SHILLING PIECE.

FOUR PENCE See GROAT.

FOUR-POUND PIECE James VI of Scotland issued this gold coin in 1580. Its design was a boyish portrait of the King on the obverse and a crowned Scottish shield on the reverse surrounded by the legend EXVRGAT DEVS ET DISSIPENTVR INIMICI EIVS ("Let God arise and let His enemies be scattered") from Psalm 68, v. 1. It was also known as the ducat (*q.v.*).

FOUR-SHILLING PIECE   See DOUBLE FLORIN and SIX-TEEN-SHILLING PIECE.

FR, FRA, FRAN, FRANC   In connection with the words REX or REGINA, these abbreviations of the Latin FRANCIAE, meaning King or Queen of France, appeared in the legend of British coins until 1801, when all claims to the French throne were relinquished. It was in use continually from the reign of Edward III, apart from the years 1360 to 1369, when the quarrel between the English and the French was patched up, and on the pattern coins of Oliver Cromwell. Although Edward had claimed the throne of France since 1337, the title did not appear on his silver coins until 1351. However, his first public declaration of being King of France was seen in 1344, on his very first gold coinage of the florin, leopard and helm.

G

GALLEY HALFPENCE These base silver coins, also known as 'janes', were imported illegally from Italy in the fifteenth century. They were basically a copy of the English halfpenny and circulated as such, although they were worth intrinsically less. The name originated from their being brought to this country by galley men or wine merchants.

GARTER COINAGE This term denotes those gold and silver coins of George III from 1816 to 1820 whose reverse designs were surrounded by the Order of the Garter – HONI SOIT QUI MAL Y PENSE.

GEORGE NOBLE In 1526, Cardinal Wolsey, the Chancellor of the Exchequer to Henry VIII, instituted a monetary reform which included the revaluation of the angel to 7s. 6d. ($37\frac{1}{2}$p). To replace the angel at the old value of 6s. 8d. ($33\frac{1}{2}$p.), the gold George noble was introduced. However, this new piece only weighed 71 grains of standard gold (23 carats $3\frac{1}{2}$ grains) as opposed to the 80 grains of the angel, the latter retaining the same weight at the new value.

24a. George Noble (obverse), and ×2

24b. George Noble (reverse), and ×2

The obverse of the George noble showed the King's titles around a Tudor rose superimposed on the side of a ship, with the initials of Henry and his first wife, Catherine of Aragon, to the left and right of the cross above. The reverse had the equestrian figure of St George slaying the dragon, hence its name. The legend surrounding this motif read TALI DICATA SIGNO MENS FLVCTVARI NEQVIT ("Consecrated by such a sign, the mind cannot waver".)

The George noble was only struck until 1533 and is a very rare coin. The half George noble, similar in all respects to the large piece, is even scarcer, for only one specimen is known.

GHOST PENNY   This was the familiar name given to pennies of George V from 1911 to 1927. For several reasons, including poor workmanship and the size of the effigy, the obverse showed through on to the reverse, giving it a ghost-like appearance.

See also MODIFIED EFFIGY.

GODLESS FLORIN   This first British silver florin (*q.v.*) was only issued in 1849. Circulation ceased almost immediately because of the absence of the inscription DEI GRATIA FID. DEF., even in abbreviated form. The omission of this religious title caused such a public outcry that the Royal Mint had to recall the coins. The Deputy Master of the Mint was made responsible for the error and he was eventually dismissed. The irreligious nature of the coin was also thought to be one of the causes of an outbreak of cholera in the same year.

25. Godless Florin (obverse and reverse)

The Godless florin resembled the Gothic crown (*q.v.*) in design, but had plain lettering. Both coins were engraved by the same artists. The florin was the first coin to show the coin's value twice in words, namely ONE FLORIN, ONE TENTH OF A POUND around the design on the reverse.

GOLD   In 1257 Henry III issued England's first gold coin, which was a gold penny worth twenty silver ones. The next gold coinage was struck in 1344, in the reign of Edward III, and gold coins were a regular feature of English and British currency until 1914, when they ceased to circulate after the appearance of Treasury notes. Sovereigns and other denominations in smaller numbers have been minted since that date and though they are legal tender they are never used, as the intrinsic metal value is higher than the value of the coin.

The first gold piece was pure, but all later issues have contained a small amount of another metal, usually copper, to give the coin the hardness necessary to keep it in circulation for a reasonable time. The present ratio is 11 parts of gold to 1 of copper.

From 1947 to 1979 the Exchange Control Act imposed certain restrictions on the residents of the United Kingdom with regard to the buying, selling and holding of gold. One point on which the Act remained unchanged was that dealing with gold bullion. Residents of the United Kingdom, except for authorized dealers (*i.e.*, all authorized banks and two further members of the London Bullion Market) or those who used gold for industrial purposes, were not permitted to hold gold bullion in the United Kingdom or abroad.

The Act of 1947 did allow genuine coin collectors to buy, sell or hold gold coins minted in or prior to 1816, provided that the value of the pieces was higher than the gold content, and they were bought and sold accordingly. In 1966 the order was changed and a restriction was placed on gold coins minted after 1837. Residents needed permission from the Bank of England to exchange or hold such coins, unless they already held no more than four before the amendment came into force. In 1971 this restriction was removed and any gold coins could be purchased, sold, or held without permission being required. Transactions involving gold coins could still be made between residents of the United Kingdom but after 1975 they were no longer allowed to buy gold coins minted after 1837 from non-residents. In October 1979 Exchange Control was abolished and now there are no longer any restrictions on persons holding or dealing in gold in any form.

See also CROWN GOLD and STANDARD GOLD.

GOLD PENNY   This coin was introduced by Henry III in 1257, and was the first piece to be struck in gold since the *thrymsa* of Saxon times. At the time, the ratio of gold to silver was ten to one and as the gold penny weighed as much as two silver ones (45 grains) it was the equivalent of twenty in value. It was minted to rival the Italian florin, which had been struck since 1252, but failed, for Britain did not have the volume of trade to warrant a gold coinage at the time. Also the coin was worth more and although the King revalued it at twenty-four silver pennies in 1265, many examples were exported or melted down.

26a. Gold Penny (obverse), and × 2

26b. Gold Penny (reverse), and × 2

The workmanship on the gold penny was superior to that on silver ones. The obverse had a full length facing portrait of the King seated on a throne with a sceptre and orb, within the legend HENRICVS REX III. The reverse showed a large cross with rosettes and pellets in the angles.

GOLD STANDARD   This standard was adopted by Great Britain in 1816 after the Napoleonic Wars. It meant that only gold coins contained their intrinsic metal value and therefore silver became only a token currency, *i.e.*, the metal in each coin would be less than its face value. A monometallic standard removed any complications which might arise in a bimetallic system where one or both metals could fluctuate in value at any time and the relationship between the two would have to be altered accordingly. On the gold standard the legal tender limit of silver coin in a transaction was set at £2. The gold standard was abandoned in this country in 1931.

GOTHIC CROWN   The name for this coin came from the design and the early English lettering which reflected the Gothic revival of the era. It was issued in 1847 and a few proofs were struck in 1853 for sets. The obverse, by William Wyon, showed a crowned bust of Queen Victoria with a richly embroidered gown around her shoulders. (This was the first crowned portrait of a monarch since Charles II.) The reverse, by W. Dyce, had the four shields of the royal arms crowned in cruciform, with the emblems, rose, thistle, and shamrock in the angles, the Star of the

Garter in the centre and all within a tressure of arcs. Around this was the legend TUEATUR UNITA DEUS ("May God guard the united") and the date in Roman numerals with ANNO DOM.

27. Gothic Crown (obverse and reverse)

GOTHIC FLORIN   This was the name given to the second series of British silver florins issued from 1851 to 1887. Like its predecessor, the 'godless florin,' it was similar in design to the Gothic crown but this time the obverse legend was in early

28. Gothic Florin of 1852 (obverse)

English lettering and included the date in Roman numerals. The Gothic florin was struck on a broader and thinner flan than the 'godless'.

GRACELESS FLORIN   Another name for the 'godless florin' (*q.v.*).

GRAINING The milled or serrated edge on silver coins was first introduced during the reign of Charles II to prevent clipping. Another term is *milling*.

GROAT The Latin *denarii grossi* gave the name to these thick coins that were first struck in the Middle Ages. *Denarii* themselves were thin coins. England's first issue appeared in 1279 in the reign of Edward I. This coin was an imitation of the *gros tournois* of Louis IX and Philip III of France, which was issued twenty years before its English counterpart at the Abbey of St Martin Tours. The English name is a corruption of the two French words for the coin which showed the Tours Abbey rather than the royal portrait.

The English groat of fourpence (1½p.) was similar to the penny in design. It consisted of a facing portrait of the king in a quatrefoil on the obverse and a long cross fleury with pellets in the angles on the reverse. As regards the legend, this coin was the first to show the inscription DEI GRATIA and the titles ᴅOMINVS HIBERNIAE ET DVX AQVITANIAS (Lord of Ireland and Duke of Aquitaine) even if in abbreviated form.

29. Groat of 1279 (obverse and reverse)

English trade had no real need for a coin above the value of a penny and the minting was discontinued. However, it was re-introduced in 1351 in the reign of Edward III, together with the half-groat. The new groat weighed only 72 grains of silver as opposed to the 89 grains of its predecessor, the reason being that the penny had been reduced from 22¼ to 18 grains during that period. This fourpenny piece was similar to the first except that it also included an inscription in two bands on the reverse, namely POSVI DEVM ADIVTOREM MEVM ("I have made God my helper") from Psalm 54, v. 4.

The groat now became a permanent feature of the coinage and was minted by most monarchs. By the time of Elizabeth I the groat was beginning to be called the fourpence but after the introduction of milled coinage in 1662 the fourpence gradually disappeared from normal circulation and was minted solely for use in the Maundy ceremony, although some experts doubt this considering the amount of circulation that these coins have seen. However, those pieces minted in the nineteenth century and after are found in such good condition that it is safe to assume that the fourpence was no longer used in everyday transactions but was reserved for the Maundy. The groat still survives today in this context as the Maundy fourpence.

The English sovereigns also struck groats for Ireland and these coins resembled those issued on the mainland. In Scotland groats were minted by the Scottish monarchs from David II (1329–71) to Mary (1542–67) and circulated for a number of values from 4d. (1½p.) to 1s. 6d. (7½p.). The first Scottish groat, slightly lighter than the English, appeared in 1367, and although the reverse was similar to the English version even down to the inscription DEVS PROTECTOR MEVS LIBERATOR MEVS ("God is my protector and liberator") the obverse favoured a profile portrait of the king with a sceptre. However, later groats reverted to the full face bust. James V (1513–42) reintroduced the profile bust for his groat, which was valued at 1s. 6d. (7½p.), but his daughter Mary dispensed with a portrait on hers which went by the names of *nonsunt* or *twelvepenny groat* (*q.v.*).

See also BRITANNIA GROAT, ONE-THIRD GROAT, TWELVE-PENNY GROAT and WOLSEY GROAT.

GUERNSEY   Although the Channel Island of Guernsey has been in the possession of the English Crown since the Norman Conquest of 1066, the currency of France remained the money of account until as late as 1921. French and English money circulated on an equal basis until that date, but Guernsey has also had a coinage of her own since 1830. The first issues were the copper one and four doubles. The eight doubles appeared in 1834 and the two doubles in 1858.

The name 'double' came from the French coin *double tournois*, which circulated on the island in the eighteenth century and which was worth about half a farthing. Consequently, the one double was the equivalent of this amount. However, although the eight doubles was the counterpart of the English penny, it was worth slightly less than the English coin, for twenty-one Guernsey shillings were needed to equal an English pound. It was not until 1921 that the exchange system was simplified and the eight doubles was equated with the English penny.

30.   (*top row*) Eight Doubles (obverse and reverse); (*bottom row*) Ten Shillings (obverse and reverse)

Apart from allowing French money to circulate on the island, Guernsey also retained the influence of her southern neighbour in the spelling of her name. The word GUERNESEY appeared on the obverse of her coins until 1949. The early coins of Guernsey were extremely simple. The obverse of the eight doubles showed the name of the island above the shield of three lions passant guardant enclosed in a wreath, the reverse showed the value and date enclosed in a wreath. The three smaller coins were similar except for the absence of the wreath on both sides of the coin.

In 1864, following the example of Great Britain, Guernsey began to use bronze instead of copper coins, which were finally demonetized in 1869. No other great change on the coins them-

selves was to be seen until the reign of Elizabeth II, when a new
design was introduced for the eight and four doubles (the one
double had last been minted in 1938, the two doubles in 1929).
The reverses retained the island's shield, but the obverses
showed the English spelling of the island, *i.e.*, GUERNSEY, the
date and denomination. In addition, the eight doubles had three
Guernsey lilies and the four doubles had one.

The reign of Elizabeth II also saw the introduction of the
island's first cupro-nickel coin; a threepence with a scalloped
edge and a picture of a Guernsey cow on the obverse. This coin
was first issued in 1956, but since it was too light, the weight was
increased for the next striking in 1959. To commemorate the
nine hundred years of British rule in 1966, Guernsey also struck
a square cupro-nickel ten-shilling piece which depicted William
the Conqueror on one side and Elizabeth II on the other.

Since 1971 Guernsey has had her own six decimal coins, identical in denomination, size and metal composition to their British
counterparts. The obverse of each showed the arms of the island
and the reverse a variety of designs: the fifty new pence, the cap of
the Duke of Normandy; the ten new pence, the Guernsey cow;
the five new pence, the Guernsey lily as on the earlier four
doubles; the two new pence, Sark mill; and the new penny a
gannet in flight. The half new penny had no design except for the
denomination. The word 'new' in the value was first dropped on
the regular issues of the ten, five and two pence pieces of 1977.

In 1972 a twenty-five pence coin was struck to commemorate
the silver wedding of Queen Elizabeth II and the Duke of Edinburgh. Others have been minted since then to commemorate
royal events, and strangely these last three issues together with
the ten-shilling piece of 1966 have been the only coins ever to
show a portrait of the reigning monarch.

1981 and 1982 saw the introduction of the one pound and
twenty pence respectively. The former, slightly larger than a
penny but much thicker, had the Guernsey lily on the reverse
and the incuse inscription 'BAILIWICK OF GUERNSEY' on
the milled edge. The reverse of the seven-sided twenty pence
showed a traditional Guernsey milk can. The arms of the island
appeared on the obverses of both coins.

Guernsey's first issue of coins was produced at Boulton and
Watt's Soho Mint in Birmingham, the second by the Brum-
magen firm of Henry Jay & Co. Since 1864 all issues have been

struck at the Royal Mint except those with the mint mark H, denoting Heaton's Birmingham mint, later the Mint, Birmingham.

GUINEA   On the introduction of a gold milled coinage in 1663, a new twenty-shilling piece (£1) was struck in place of the hammered unit. This new coin was called a guinea, after Guinea in West Africa, later the Gold Coast and now Ghana. This country was the major source of gold bullion for the coins, and those pieces struck from it bore the emblem of an elephant or elephant and castle, which was the badge of the suppliers, the African Company.

The first guinea weighed $131\frac{3}{4}$ grains of 22 carat gold, but seven years later it was reduced to $129\frac{1}{2}$ grains, which remained constant until the final issue in 1813. However, the value of the guinea continued to fluctuate with the rise and fall in the price of gold. At one stage it circulated for thirty shillings (£1. 50p.), but its value was finally fixed at twenty-one shillings in 1717, when its name was also officially accepted for the first time. A century later the guinea was replaced by the twenty-shilling sovereign in the recoinage of 1816, but it still remained an official money of account until the decimalization of the currency in 1971.

31. Guinea of 1673 (obverse and reverse)

John Roettier's engraving of the guinea of Charles II was retained by later monarchs. This design consisted of a laureate truncated bust of the monarch on the obverse (the draped bust was reserved for silver coins). The reverse had the quarters of the royal arms in crowned shields, in cruciform, with sceptres in the angles. George II and George III, the last two kings to issue guineas, preferred a large crowned shield of the royal arms to the cruciform arrangement on the reverse.

See also PENINSULA GUINEA and SPADE GUINEA.

GUN MONEY   After his abdication, James II fled to France in

December 1688, but he returned only three months later in order to regain the throne from his Protestant successor, William III. He landed at Kinsale in Ireland and it soon became necessary for him to pay the Catholic troops he had collected in that country, together with those he had brought with him from France. Since the Protestants either hoarded or sent most of their gold and silver across to England because of the threat of a civil war between supporters of James and William, it meant that there was a lack of precious metal, and any that James managed to collect from his supporters was immediately sent abroad to buy arms for his Catholic troops.

To pay the army it became clear that an emergency or token coinage was necessary. This token coinage was termed 'gun money', and the denominations included half-crowns, shillings and sixpences which were struck in brass at Dublin and Limerick. The crown appeared later. It was emphasized that the coins were only temporary and would be redeemed for their value in gold and silver once James had secured the English throne again. That the coins were dated by month as well as by year suggests that James had every intention of redeeming them month by month until his debt to his supporters was paid. (At that time the New Year occurred in the middle of March and thus those dated March 1689 and March 1690 belonged to the same month.)

Supplies of brass to mint the coins soon became very low and even the requests of the French ambassador to his country to send metal went unanswered. Thus, all types of base metal had to be used, including two obsolete guns from Dublin Castle, and the same fate befell many other French and Irish cannons. The source of the metal gave rise to the name 'gun money'.

Trading difficulties with the new coinage were soon encountered when merchants would only send their goods to market if they could charge treble prices. Even James's own Lord Chancellor would not accept gun money when rents were paid. Finally, in order to retain his French troops, James had to pay them with the silver he had brought with him.

It was to William's advantage that no one had confidence in the brass coinage. When he landed in Ireland in the summer of 1689, he bought the farmers' crops with gold and silver. James's problems, however, increased. In March 1690, groats, pennies and halfpennies were struck in pewter, later a crown was struck in white metal and the brass half-crown and shilling were reduced in weight. Three months later, the half-crowns, shillings and sixpences were called in and restruck as crowns, half-crowns and shillings respectively. This was a final attempt to prevent the complete collapse of the coinage.

In the following month, on 1st July 1690, William defeated James at the Battle of the Boyne. The victor immediately reduced the gun money to its intrinsic metal value, thus rendering the coins worthless and ruining many people financially, especially James's soldiers. Each coin, depending on its weight and metal content, became worth anything from a farthing to a penny. An estimated £22,500 worth of gun money was struck and overnight it was devalued to about £600. However, Limerick continued to mint halfpennies and farthings in brass until the city finally surrendered in October 1691. The reverses of these Limerick halfpennies and farthings depicted a seated Hibernia for the first time on Irish coins.

Considering that gun money was a money of necessity, the design was of a high standard. The striking, however, was often crude. All crowns depicted James seated on a horse on the obverse and the quarters of the royal arms in quatrefoil on the reverse. The other denominations were similar, the obverses showing a bust of the dethroned king, the reverses a crown superimposed on two crossed sceptres with the value of the piece in peace and Roman numerals, the month below, and I and R (*Iacobus Rex*) to the sides. The year appeared in the legend, which surprisingly contained the title of King of France, a claim likely to cause offence to the French, upon whose help James was so dependent.

32. (*left to right*) Gun Money Crown (obverse); Gun Money Half-crown, large size (reverse)

H

H   This letter was a mint-mark that appeared on Victorian pennies, halfpennies and farthings from 1874 to 1876 and 1881 to 1882, on George V pennies in 1912, 1918 and 1919, and many other times on coins issued for other countries, mainly those belonging to the British Empire and later the Commonwealth. It

33. 1918H Penny (reverse)

signified that the pieces were made at the Heaton Mint in Birmingham, and its appearance on British coins showed that the demand on the Royal Mint was too great at the time. Heaton's Birmingham mint is now called the Mint, Birmingham.

See also MINTS.

HALF-CROWN   The half-crown was originally a gold coin issued in 1526. In nearly all respects it was a miniature of the crown of the double rose (*q.v.*), weighing half of the five-shilling piece and being minted from gold of the same fineness. In design it differed from the larger piece, in that the obverse legend contained the inscription RVTILANS ROSA SINE SPINA ("A dazzling rose without a thorn"). The king's titles were restricted to the reverse of the coin in an abbreviated form – HENRIC 8 DI. GRA. REX AGL. Z FRA.

Although this was the first true half-crown, it is necessary to point out that as early as 1464 Edward IV struck a quarter ryal which was valued at thirty pence ($12\frac{1}{2}$p.). Half-crowns circulated for the same amount until 1611, when, like the rest of the coinage, its value was raised by 10 per cent. The half-crowns struck from 1611 to 1619 were the last gold specimens to be minted and were issued at 2s. 9d. (14p.). During its history, the gold half-crown suffered the same fate as the crown and the Britain crown in having its weight gradually reduced. The last issues were only $19\frac{1}{4}$ grains, almost a third less than the $28\frac{3}{4}$ grains of the original coins.

By 1551 the crown was also struck as a silver coin, and its half appeared in the same year. This coin of Edward VI was a smaller version of the five-shilling piece. It had the King seated on a walking horse (on some types the horse is galloping) with the date below on the obverse and a shield of the royal arms on a cross on the reverse. The first half-crowns weighed 240 grains but this was reduced to $232\frac{1}{4}$ grains for the next issue which appeared in 1601 in the reign of Elizabeth I. Elizabeth's successor, James I, was the first to show the value on the coin itself, namely XXX, representing thirty pence.

After the introduction of a milled coinage in the reign of Charles II, the design on the half-crown became standardized. In various forms the royal coat of arms appeared on most issues and in the last years of Britain's duodecimal currency it was the only coin to feature that motif.

34. Half-crown of 1664 (obverse and reverse)

There are a few points to note in the later history of the half-crown, which, since its inception, was struck in every reign except those of Mary, and Philip and Mary. In the great recoinage of 1816, the weight of the coin was decreased to 218 grains but the silver fineness was maintained. Later in the same century, from 1851 to 1873, no half-crowns were struck as the government of the day was contemplating decimalization and the florin had been introduced to replace them. The idea was, shelved, however, until the 1960s, and in preparation for the new decimal coinage the half-crown was last struck for general circulation with the date 1967. By this time the coin was minted in cupro-nickel which, in 1947, replaced the 50 per cent silver alloy that had been in use since 1920.

The half-crown was demonetized on 1st January 1970. Proof specimens dated 1970 were later issued together with other £. s. d. coins for collectors.

HALF DOLLAR   The four-real Spanish coin of Charles III or Charles IV was countermarked with an oval stamp which showed the portrait of George III, and was issued in 1797 for 2s. 4½d. (approx. 12p.).

See DOLLAR.

HALF-FARTHING   This tiny copper coin, only eighteen millimetres in diameter, was issued in the reigns of George IV, William IV and Victoria. The earlier types were a smaller version of the penny with a Britannia reverse, but those of Victoria showed the value written in two lines with a crown above and the date

35. Half-farthing (reverse)

below. The half-farthing was struck especially for Ceylon but became legal tender in Great Britain in 1842 and remained so until it was demonetized together with the rest of the copper coinage in 1870.

See also PATRICK.

HALF-GROAT   See TWOPENCE.

HALF-GUINEA   The gold half-guinea was struck regularly from 1669 (in the reign of Charles II) to 1813 (when George III was on the throne), when it was superseded by the half-sovereign.

See also GUINEA.

HALF-MERK This was first struck in 1572, in debased silver two-thirds fine. It was worth 6s. 8d. (33½p.) in Scottish money and was therefore also called a noble. The obverse showed the numerals 6 and 8 on either side of a Scottish shield, the reverse showed four I's, crowned, in the shape of a cross with a five-pointed star in the centre and crowns and thistleheads alternatively in the angles. The inscription around the reverse was SALVVM FAC POPVLVM TVVM DOMINE ("O Lord, save Thy people") from Psalm 28, v. 9. The half-merk was struck until 1580, when James VI issued a finer silver coinage. A quarter-merk or half-noble was also issued in the same coinage. It differed from the half-merk only in that a 3 and 4 represented the value, replacing the 6 and 8.

The half-merk of Charles I displayed the figures VI and 8 behind the King's portrait, and that of Charles II bore the same in the centre of the cruciform shields on the reverse. The inscription around the royal arms on the reverse of the noble of Charles I read CHRISTO AVSPICE REGNO ("I reign under the auspices of God"). The coins of Charles II belonged to the milled coinage, which is noted for its lack of inscriptions. The last half-merk was struck in 1675.

Smaller denominations of the Charles I series were called forty- and twenty-penny pieces (*q.v.*) while the Charles II half-merk was the smallest coin in the merk group.

HALF NEW PENNY The smallest decimal coin appeared, together with the rest of the bronze pieces, on 15th February 1971, when the decimal currency was introduced in Great Britain. The obverse showed Arnold Machin's portrait of Elizabeth II, and the reverse a crown with the figure ½ below. From 1982 the word 'NEW' was omitted.

HALFPENNY The first record of a round halfpenny being minted in England was about the year A.D. 875 when the Danish King Halfdene struck such a coin while he was occupying the city of London. The obverse of this silver piece bore the name of the king and the reverse showed the monogram of London. It is thought to be a copy of the penny of Alfred the Great.

Until 1278 halfpennies were struck irregularly and then only in small quantities for it was usually easier to make a halfpenny by cutting a penny in half along one of the arms of the cross. This method, however, was unreliable as it was almost impossible to ascertain whether one had been short-changed or not, even when the cross allowed for an equal cutting which could only be undertaken by an official moneyer.

Edward I instituted a recoinage in 1279 in an effort to improve the currency and he introduced a round, silver halfpenny which was again a copy of the penny. Henry I had attempted to issue a round halfpenny as early as 1108 but it is considered that the high cost of production at the time aroused the moneyers' opposition to the coin.

The halfpenny of Edward I became a popular coin but as time went by the price of silver increased and accordingly the piece became smaller, with the result that it proved impossible to be minted economically after the reign of Charles I. After being struck first in 11 grains of silver in 1280, the halfpenny weighed a mere $3\frac{3}{4}$ grains by 1601. The size of these coins is reflected in the design. There was not enough space to show any legend or bust of Queen Elizabeth I. The obverse had only a portcullis; the reverse a cross and pellets.

After the restoration of the monarchy, plans for a copper coinage were made and in 1672 the first regal issues of copper halfpennies and farthings appeared with a portrait of Charles II on the obverse and Britannia on the reverse. James II and William and Mary struck tin halfpennies with a small plug of copper in the centre to prevent counterfeiting, but poor durability of this metal meant that production in copper was resumed in 1694.

36. Halfpenny of 1957 (obverse and reverse)

Britannia held her position on the reverse of the halfpenny until the 1936 bronze issue (from 1860 bronze had replaced copper) and the following year she was superseded by a design of Drake's ship, the *Golden Hind*, by T. H. Paget. On 1st August 1969 the halfpenny was demonetized in preparation for the introduction of decimal currency in 1971. Although 1967 was the last date on a halfpenny for general circulation, specimens dated 1970 appeared in the £.s.d. proof sets of that year.

There is a legend about the first round halfpennies of Edward I. With this new denomination the King is supposed to have fulfilled the prophecy of King Arthur's magician, Merlin, who foretold the end of an independent Wales when the English sovereign "made his money round", which indeed happened.

HALF-SHILLING   See Sixty-shilling Piece.

HALF-SOVEREIGN   The half-sovereign first appeared as a gold coin in the third coinage of Henry VIII in 1545. It was a smaller version of the sovereign (*q.v.*) weighing 96 grains of 22 carat gold, and was worth 10s. (50p.). It was struck in the reigns of Edward VI and James VI, and also Elizabeth, when it was called a half-pound. By this time it weighed 10 grains less than the original issue.

In 1604 the name of the ten-shilling piece was changed to double crown, which was later replaced by the half-guinea. The term *half-sovereign* re-emerged after the recoinage of 1816, and the coin was struck regularly from 1817 to 1926 at a new, lighter weight of $61\frac{3}{4}$ grains. Two proof issues were made in the coronation years of George VI and Elizabeth II, the latter being produced expressly for official collections. In 1980 a proof half-sovereign was minted and sold on its own or in sets with £5, £2, and sovereign pieces. It was struck again in 1982.

HALF-UNITE   See Double Crown.

HAMMERED COINS   *Hammered* means that such coins were struck by hand. A piece of metal was placed between two dies and the upper one, the trussel or trustle, was struck with a hammer onto the lower one, the pile which was wedged in a block of wood. The pile usually bore the obverse of a coin; the trussel the reverse. In 1662 this slow process was abandoned in favour of a milled coinage struck on machines. The machines not only had the advantage of producing coins more quickly but also could turn out regularly shaped pieces. Hammered coins were demonetized in 1697.

HANOVER JACKS   See Cumberland Jacks.

HARDHEAD   This billon coin, the name of which is a corruption of the French piece, *hardi* or *hardit*, was issued in Scotland in the reigns of Mary and her son, James VI, before he became King of England in 1603. A half-hardhead was struck in the latter's reign.

A hardhead was also called a lion because of the reverse design of a crowned lion rampant, but it is not to be confused with the Scottish gold coin of the same name (*q.v.*). The lion was encircled by the inscription VICIT VERITAS (Truth has conquered) or VINCIT VERITAS (Truth conquers). The obverses had the sovereign's monogram crowned.

The hardhead weighed $14\frac{3}{4}$ grains and circulated for $1\frac{1}{2}$d. (approx. $\frac{1}{2}$p.), and later for 2d. (approx 1p.). The weight of the higher value coins of James VI had been raised to $23\frac{1}{2}$ grains, but they contained less than five per cent silver.

HARP   The emblem first appeared on Irish coins in the sixteenth century and has done so regularly ever since that time. It has been the obverse design of all £.s.d. and decimal denominations of the Irish Free State and the Republic of Ireland since 1928, except for the commemorative ten-shilling piece of 1966.

HARRINGTON FARTHING   In 1613 James I granted a licence to Lord Harrington of Exton in Rutland to strike copper farthings on the condition that they would share the profits. This was to stop the circulation of halfpenny and farthing tokens issued by shopkeepers at the time. However, it is noticeable that James did not allow the Mint to produce coins in a base metal which would show his portrait, although the 'Harringtons' do bear his titles.

37a. Harrington Farthing (obverse), and $\times 2\frac{1}{2}$

37b. Harrington Farthing (reverse), and ×2½

The obverse showed a crown superimposed on crossed sceptres within the legend IACO D.G. MAG. BRIT.; the reverse a crowned Irish harp surrounded by FRA. ET HIB. REX.

To give the coins a silver appearance the first issues were tin-plated. This practice was later abandoned and the size of the untinned farthings was slightly increased.

After the death of Lord Harrington in 1614 the licence was obtained from Lady Harrington by the Duke of Lennox.

HAT PIECE   This gold coin of almost 70 grains of 22 carat gold was circulated for eighty Scottish shillings (£4), from 1591 to 1593, by James VI of Scotland. The ducat received this name from the obverse design which depicted the King, facing right,

38.   Hat Piece (obverse and reverse)

wearing a very tall hat. The reverse design was just as unusual in that it showed a lion seated on a throne and holding a sceptre which it pointed to a cloud. Above the cloud the word *Jehovah* was written in Hebrew and the Latin legend surrounding this design was TE SOLVM VEREOR ("The above I do fear").

HELM   This was the name of the gold quarter-florin issued by Edward III in 1344, and was so called on account of the obverse design of a helmet surmounted by a crowned lion on a field of fleur-de-lis. This was surrounded by the King's titles. The reverse showed a simpler floriate cross than on the leopard and florin. Here the inscription was EXALTABITVR IN GLORIA ("He shall be exalted in glory") from Psalm 112, v. 9.

The helm weighed 27 grains of 23 carat $3\frac{1}{2}$ grains fine gold

39. Helm (obverse), and $\times 2\frac{1}{2}$

and was worth 1s. 6d. ($7\frac{1}{2}$p.). Like the florin and the leopard (*q.v.*) it was only issued once and was replaced in the same year by the quarter noble.

HI., HIB., HIBER., HYB.   In connection with the words REX or REGINA, these abbreviations of the Latin HIBER-NIAE, meaning Ireland, appeared on English and British coins until 1801, and referred to the monarch's claim to that country. From Edward I to Henry VIII, the abbreviations were used with DOMINVS (Latin for 'lord') or the letters DNS. Henry VIII decided to change his title from Lord to King of Ireland in 1542. King John, the first ruler of Ireland, only used the letters DOM to designate his title received from his father. From 1801 BRI-TANNIARUM REX included King of England, Scotland and Ireland.

HIBERNIA   Just as Britannia is the symbol of England, Hibernia is the female figure representing Ireland, a seated lady in long flowing robes with a harp at her side.

40. Halfpenny of William Wood (reverse) showing Hibernia

INCHIQUIN MONEY   Inchiquin money is the name given to a series of irregularly shaped pieces of gold and silver with the weight stamped on them that appeared in Ireland during the Civil War. They were considered to have been minted for Charles I by Murrough O'Brien, Lord Inchiquin and Vice-President of Munster, from plate donated by Irish royalists. However, evidence now suggests that they were issued by the Lord Justices of Ireland and were never authorized by the King.

41. Inchiquin Pistole (obverse and reverse)

The silver coins struck in 1642 included the crown, half-crown, shilling, ninepence, sixpence, fourpence, and threepence. The rare gold pistoles and double pistoles which did not appear until 1646 have the distinction of being the only gold coins minted in or for Ireland.

IND. IMP.   The title denoting *Indiae Imperator* or *Imperatrix* (Emperor or Empress of India) first appeared on English coins in 1893 on the issue of the 'veiled head' coinage of Victoria. Queen Victoria had been proclaimed Empress of India as early as 1877, but the title was not added to the legend on her coinage until later. When India became a republic in 1947, George VI relinquished the title and the IND. IMP. was omitted from all legends in 1949.

INITIALS   In former times the name or initials of the moneyer often appeared on the coins he struck, and they are sometimes used to allocate to a particular period a coin which bears no date. However, since the time of George III it has been customary for an engraver to put his initials in or next to the design that has been chosen for a coin, rather like an artist signing his name below a painting. They are, to date:

W   Thomas Wyon Jr, the designer and engraver of the reverse of the 'bull-head' half-crown and engraver of Pistrucci's 'bull-head' effigy of George III.

K   Conrad Heinrich Küchler, whose designs included the 'cartwheel' pennies and twopences of George III.

BP   Benedetto Pistrucci. He is famous for the St George and the dragon reverse that has been in use since the time of George III. On the George III crown his surname appeared in full below the same design.

WWP   William Wellesley Pole, who was the brother of the Duke of Wellington and for a time Master of the Mint. Although he was not an engraver, his initials were carefully hidden in the ground line of St George and the dragon design of certain coins of George III and George IV.

JBM   Jean Baptiste Merlen, a Frenchman of Flemish origin who was responsible for reverses of certain coins of George IV and William IV.

WW   William Wyon, most famous for portraits of George IV, William IV and Victoria. The reverse of the 1839 proof five pounds showing Una and the Lion (*q.v.*) had W. Wyon R.A.

LCW   Leonard Charles Wyon, most famous for the 'bun' portrait on Victorian bronze coins, and the Britannia reverse.

JEB   Sir Joachim Edgar Boehm, who engraved the obverses of the jubilee coins of Victoria.

TB   Thomas Brock, responsible for the 'veiled head' issues of Victoria.

DeS   G. W. de Saulles. He designed the coinage of Edward VII.

BM   Sir Bertram Mackennal, whose work included the portrait of George V but no reverses of the coins.

PM   Percy Metcalfe, whose initials appeared below the modernistic design of St George and the Dragon on the 1935 crown of George V.

KG   George Kruger Gray, who produced designs for reverses of certain coins of George VI and later pieces of George

V, as well as the unissued coinage of Edward VIII.

HP   Thomas Humphrey Paget, whose work included the portraits of Edward VIII and George VI. He was also the designer of the *Golden Hind* halfpenny of George VI, a motif originally intended for the half-crown but rejected.

WP   H. Wilson Parker. His design of the wren was accepted for the farthing of George VI and Elizabeth II.

MG   Mary Gillick. Her portrait of Elizabeth II was retained until the decimal coins were introduced.

WG   W. Gardner, responsible for the portcullis on the reverse of the threepence of Elizabeth II.

EF·CT Edgar Fuller and Cecil Thomas, who together produced the reverses of the half-crown, florin and sixpence, as well as the crown of 1953 and 1960 for Elizabeth II.

GL   Gilbert Ledward. He designed the obverse of the 1953 Coronation crown of Elizabeth II.

For biographical notes on some designers see PISTRUCCI and WYON. See also ENGRAVERS.

IRELAND   The earliest known coins to have been issued in Ireland were those that circulated around Dublin under the auspices of the Viking invaders who had settled there at the beginning of the eleventh century, during the reign of Sihtric II. The coins, imitations of those issued by Aethelred II in England, soon lacked the high standard of workmanship which was seen on the early pieces, and at the end of the series in about 1150 they were crude in style and light in weight.

Between 1177 and 1205, John de Courcey, a Norman nobleman and self-styled Lord of Ulster, issued halfpennies and farthings which today are quite rare. The first Anglo-Irish pieces, consisting of badly struck halfpennies and farthings in debased silver, were put into circulation by Henry II in the name of his son John, who had received the title of Lord of Ireland following the capture of the eastern part of Ireland by the Earl of Pembroke for the King. When John eventually came to the throne, he also struck a series of pennies which showed his portrait in a triangle rather than a circle, a device which was retained until the reign of Edward III. The three denominations continued to be circulated in small issues during the reigns of some kings until 1460, when Edward IV approved the striking of a higher denomination – the groat. Following the huge rise in the price of silver, he later introduced the double groat or eightpence (*q.v.*). In Edward's reign the island's first base metal coinage appeared, consisting of brass farthings on which St Patrick was featured for the first time on Irish coins.

Two years after Henry VII's accession to the English throne and the beginning of the Tudor dynasty, the Yorkist supporters in Ireland, whom Henry had defeated, issued some groats which have been attributed to Lambert Simnel, whom they wanted to put on the throne as Edward VI. The later Tudor monarchs and James I issued silver and billon shillings, sixpences and three-pences for Ireland. The Irish coins of Charles I and James II are characterized by various monies of necessity or emergency monies (*q.v.*) and gun money respectively.

After James II's defeat very few coins were struck especially for Ireland, and this caused an acute shortage of small change, particularly under the Hanoverian kings. In fact, from the time of Charles II, all coins were minted in base metal and, gun money excluded, the only denominations were penny, halfpenny and farthing.

At the turn of the eighteenth century the Irish rejected Wood's issue of copper coins (*q.v.*) and tokens appeared when official issues were not made. By the beginning of the following century, Irish coins were worth less than their English counterparts – thirteen Irish pennies equalling an English shilling. The last Anglo-Irish issues appeared in 1823, when the union with England was confirmed, and three years later Irish coins were demonetized, British pieces being the only ones which were legal tender from then on.

Before passing to the modern issues, mention should be made of the Bank of England silver tokens for the values of six shillings, thirty pence, tenpence and fivepence which were issued in the reign of George III.

When she achieved her independence in 1928, the Irish Free State or the Republic of Ireland decided to issue her own currency but to use British denominations. A committee, under the chairmanship of the poet W. B. Yeats, chose the animal designs of Percy Metcalfe: the horse on the half-crown, the salmon on the florin, the bull on the shilling, the greyhound on the sixpence, the rabbit on the threepence, the hen and chickens on the penny, the pig and piglets on the halfpenny and the woodcock on the farthing. The date across the centre of the obverse was split by the Irish harp and legend was SAORSTAT EIREANN (Gaelic for Irish Free State). After becoming a republic in 1937, the name on the coins was changed to EIRE on issues after 1939, and the date was placed to the right of the harp.

42. (*top row*) Irish Half Crown (obverse and reverse); (*bottom row*) Irish Penny (obverse and reverse)

In 1966 a silver-copper ten-shilling piece, Eire's first commemorative coin, was struck to mark the fiftieth anniversary of the 1916 Easter uprising, when a provisional republican government was set up in Dublin. The coin was designed by T. Humphrey Paget who is well known for his work on the British coinage of George VI. The obverse showed the poet and scholar, Padraig H. Pears, who led the rebellion against the British and read out the declaration of independence to the people from the steps of the Post Office in Dublin. He was later executed with other rebels after their surrender. The reverses had Cuchulainn, a legendary Irish hero, modelled after a sculpture by Olivair Sheppard. The piece was unpopular, possibly because ten shillings was a new coin denomination and people preferred the paper banknote, and so it was called in by the government to be melted down. However, of the two million coins minted, about 750,000 are officially missing, presumably in the hands of collectors.

Following Britain's lead, Ireland decided to introduce a decimal currency in 1971, each denomination and size being the same as its British counterpart. With regard to the designs, the harp obverse was retained and three animals remained on the cupro-nickel coins; the woodcock, the salmon and the bull, on the fifty, ten and fivepence respectively. The designs on the copper issues by Miss Gabriel Hayes were adaptations of illuminations; the halfpenny from a manuscript in Cologne Cathedral library; the one penny from the Book of Kells; and the twopence from the second Bible of Charles the Bald in the National Library in Paris.

See also VOCE POPULI, ST PATRICK'S MONEY, ARMSTRONG FARTHING, GUN MONEY and EMERGENCY MONEY.

J

JACOBUS   This is another name for the unite of James I.

JANE   See GALLEY HALFPENNY.

JERSEY   The years 1841, 1866 and 1877 are perhaps the three most important dates in the early history of the coinage of Jersey. Late in the first half of the nineteenth century it was decided to replace the French money that had been in use on the island until that time with British currency. The Jersey penny was equated with two French *sous*, two hundred and sixty of which were needed to make a British pound. It therefore follows that thirteen Jersey pennies equalled one shilling and this accounts for the peculiar denominations of a thirteenth, twenty-sixth and fifty-second of a shilling which appeared in 1841. Corresponding adjustments were made in the weight of these penny, halfpenny and farthing coins and twenty-six Jersey pennies were minted from a pound of copper, as opposed to twenty-four British ones. In 1866 Jersey followed the example of the British base metal currency six years earlier and changed from copper to the more durable bronze. In 1877 the three values were altered to a twelfth, twenty-fourth and forty-eighth of a shilling, so that everything would be less complicated.

43a.   One Thirteenth of a Shilling (obverse and reverse)

The obverses of Jersey's coins have always shown the head of the reigning British monarch. Although there was no distinction between the effigy on the copper issues of Jersey and Britain, the bronze pieces have always shown the monarch wearing a crown (a coronet in the case of Victoria). The portraits have been identical to those on issues of the British Empire and Commonwealth. Since decimalization the Arnold Machin portrait has been used, as on British coins. The reverses of the island's coins have always depicted the Jersey shield of three lions passant guardant in various designs, together with the date, denomination and legend STATES OF JERSEY. To commemorate the liberation of the island in 1945, a special issue of the penny was made, the legend ISLAND OF JERSEY replacing the earlier one. These coins were issued in 1949, 1950, 1952 and 1954 and although they all have the date 1945, the last issue is easily distinguished from the rest because the portrait of Elizabeth II replaced the effigy of her father George VI. In 1957 the name was changed again, this time to BAILIWICK OF JERSEY, which appeared on the twelfth of a shilling and the new round threepence in nickel-brass which was called a quarter of a shilling. Later issues of this quarter of a shilling, in 1964 and 1966, were duodecagonal like the British threepence.

43b. One Twelfth of a Shilling of 1945 (obverse and reverse)

In the last few years prior to decimalization in 1971, most of Jersey's coins were commemorative by nature. In addition to the liberation pennies, the 1960 twelfth of a shilling celebrated the restoration of the English monarchy in 1660, and the 1966 coins (twelfth of a shilling, quarter of a shilling, and a new denomination, the cupro-nickel crown) celebrated the anniversary of the Norman Conquest nine hundred years before. For the silver wedding of Queen Elizabeth II and the Duke of Edinburgh, Jersey produced a series of gold and silver coins. The gold pieces included fifty, twenty-five, twenty, ten and five pounds, the silver two pounds and fifty pence, two pounds, one pound, and fifty pence. All the reverse denominations were different, each depicting a motif pertaining to Jersey culture or natural history. These were designed by Norman Sillman. A traditional crown-sized piece was struck for the silver jubilee of Queen Elizabeth II in 1977, but a two pound coin commemorated the wedding of HRH Prince Charles and Lady Diana Spencer in 1981.

Jersey changed to a decimal currency at the same time as Great Britain in 1971. The denominations are identical to their British counterparts and are minted to the same standards in size, weight and metal composition. Each obverse has the Queen's portrait and QUEEN ELIZABETH THE SECOND, and all the reverses the arms of Jersey with BAILIWICK OF JERSEY above and the value in words and the date below. The word 'NEW' was omitted from the values of the regular issues in 1981 although it had not appeared on the fifty pence of 1972 nor on the 1977 twenty-five pence.

In 1981 a pound coin was struck for general circulation. This piece was square with camfered corners, similar to Guernsey ten shillings of 1966 (*q.v.*). The obverse had the portrait of Queen Elizabeth II, the reverse the cap badge of the Jersey militia with the commemorative inscription BICENTENARY OF THE BATTLE OF JERSEY. The edge had plain and grained sections. 1982 saw the introduction of the twenty pence, a seven-sided coin like its British counterpart, with the lighthouse at La Corbière on the reverse.

JETTON   This term is used for reckoning or gaming counters.

JOEY   See BRITANNIA GROAT.

JUBILEE COINAGE   Sir Joachim Boehm designed the portrait of the queen for the new coinage which appeared in 1887, the year of Victoria's Golden Jubilee. The bust was severely criticized even though the queen was portrayed as an elderly lady, the previous effigy of her with slight modifications to show her ageing features having been in use since her accession in 1837. Objections were made to the queen's miniature crown which looked as if it would slide off her head at any moment.

The pieces included five pounds, two pounds, sovereign and half-sovereign in gold, crown, double florin, half-crown, florin, shilling, sixpence, fourpence and threepence, as well as the four Maundy coins in silver. No bronze coins bearing a jubilee portrait were minted. The double florin was a completely new de-nomination and was worth four shillings (20p.) (*q.v.*). The fourpence only appeared in 1888 and was minted especially for use in British Guiana (now Guyana).

44. Jubilee Head Sovereign of Victoria (obverse), and ×2

The sovereign and the half retained the designs of previous issues, namely, St George and the Dragon and a shield of the royal arms respectively. The five and two pounds also had the St George and the Dragon reverse, as did the silver crown. The other larger silver pieces showed the royal arms in various forms; the double florin and florin in cruciform, the half-crown the complete shield encircled by the garter and collar of the Order of the Garter. The collar was omitted from around the shield on the shilling and sixpence. The 'young head' reverses on the four-pence, threepence and Maundy coins were retained for the jubilee issue.

The shilling was the only coin on which a change was made on the obverse. In 1889 the portrait of the queen was enlarged. The sixpence had two reverse designs. It was found that if it was gilded it looked similar to the half-sovereign and could pass as such. It was, therefore, withdrawn after only six months' circula-tion and the shield was replaced by an oak and laurel wreath motif, with the words SIX PENCE enclosed within it and a crown above. This was, in fact, a return to the 'young head' design.

The jubilee coinage designs were discontinued in 1893 in favour of the 'veiled head' issue (*q.v.*).

K

KILKENNY MONEY   This is the name given to an emergency money struck at Kilkenny, Ireland, in 1642 by the Confederated Catholics who desired religious freedom and proclaimed loyalty to the king. The issue consisted of poorly struck halfpennies and farthings. They resembled the Richmond and Maltravers farthings which circulated throughout the British Isles under royal licence, and showed a crown and two crossed sceptres on the obverse and a crowned harp between C.R. on the reverse.

K.N.   These initials appeared on the 1918 and 1919 pennies of George V, and denoted that the Kings Norton Metal Co. of Birmingham was responsible for striking them. Like Heaton's mint, this firm was requested to produce coins for use in Great Britain to ease the load of the Royal Mint.

See also MINTS.

45. 1918KN Penny (reverse)

L

LAUREL   The James I sovereign, or unite, of the third coinage from 1619 to 1625, was reduced in weight from 155 grains to 140½. At the same time, it was renamed a 'laurel' because of the wreath around the King's head on the obverse. The reverse design was the same as that on the unite – the royal coat of arms – and the inscription read FACIAM EOS IN GENTEM VNAM ("I shall make them into one people").

46. Laurel (obverse)

The half- and quarter-laurels were similar but here the inscription was HENRICVS ROSAS REGNA IACOBVS ("Henry united the roses, James the kingdoms").

Each coin also showed its value in shillings in Roman numerals (XX, X, or V) behind the King's portrait.

LENNOX FARTHING   The Duke of Lennox obtained the licence to mint farthings after the death of Lord Harrington. The coins were similar to Harrington's copper farthings except that they were slightly larger, the T was omitted from BRIT in the legend, which started at the top instead of 'eleven o'clock'.

On Lennox's death in 1624, the licence passed to his widow, the Duchess of Richmond. See RICHMOND FARTHING.

LEOPARD   The gold half-florin of Edward III, issued in 1344, was so called because a 'crowned leopard', the heraldic term for a lion with a facing head, appeared with a banner of the arms of England and France on the obverse. The reverse was the same as the florin, an elaborate cross with the end of each limb crowned within a quatrefoil. The inscription around this motif was DOMINE NE IN FVRORE TVO ARGVAS ME ("O Lord, rebuke me not in Thine anger") from Psalm 6, v.1.

47. Leopard of 1344 (obverse), and ×2

The leopard weighed 54 grains of 23 carat 3½ grains fine gold, and circulated for 3s. (15p.). It was discontinued in the same year as it was introduced, being replaced by the half-noble.

LIMA　This word appeared underneath the bust of George II on gold guineas and half-guineas, silver half-crowns, shillings and sixpences struck in 1745, and on gold five guineas and the same silver pieces, together with crowns, in 1746.

48. Shilling of 1745–46 (obverse) with LIMA inscription

During a dispute between England and Spain, which later resulted in the War of Jenkin's Ear in 1742, Admiral George Anson was equipped with a number of ships in order to harass the Spaniards. He captured a Spanish galleon coming from Acapulco and took possession of £500,000 of bullion, which he brought back to England in 1744 after circumnavigating the world.

Another story considers that the bullion arrived in England from another source. In 1745 two British privateers, *Prince Frederick* and *Duke*, took the gold and silver from some French ships which were returning home from Peru.

Whichever story is true, it is generally assumed that little, if any, of the bullion came from Lima itself, but the name of Peru's capital was suitably short to put on coins minted from a proportion of the captured wealth, to show the approximate source of the metal and commemorate the success of the British navy.

LIMERICK MONEY   See GUN MONEY.

LION   The silver denier and half-denier of the Anglo-Gallic series of Henry III bore the arms of Aquitaine and a lion, hence they are sometimes referred to as 'lion' and 'demi-lion'.

The term 'lion' was also used for a Scottish gold coin weighing $61\frac{1}{2}$ grains and valued at 5s. (25p.), which was first struck in 1390 by Robert III. Later in his reign, Robert issued a light gold coinage, and the lion was only 38 grains.

49.   Lion of James II (obverse and reverse)

The piece was minted again in the reign of James II (1437–60) when its weight was 54 grains, yet it circulated for twice the value of previous issues. Every lion had an obverse of a crowned shield and the reverse showed Scotland's patron saint crucified on a saltire cross. It is for this reason that the lion was also called a 'St Andrew'. The lions of Robert II bore the inscription XPC REGNAT XPC VINCIT XPC IMPERAT ("Christ rules, Christ conquers, Christ commands"), while the first issue of James had SALVVM FAC POPVLVM TVVM DOMINE ("O Lord, save

Thy people") from Psalm 28, v. 9, before adopting the original legend on later issues.

James IV (1488–1513) also struck two types of lion. The second type was like those of the two other kings but the first, a unique coin in itself, had a reverse of St Andrew standing and holding his cross. The lions of James IV weighed slightly less than those of James II, but had been revalued to 13s. 4d. (66½p.).

See also DEMY-LION and HARDHEAD.

LION NOBLE   From 1584 to 1588, James VI of Scotland issued a noble worth 75s. (£3.75). It weighed 78½ grains but was of a lesser fineness than many other gold coins of his reign, containing only 21½ carats. The origin of its name was the obverse design of a crowned lion seated, holding a sword and sceptre. It

50. Lion Noble (obverse and reverse)

was not unlike the lion that appeared centuries later on the Scottish shillings of George VI (1937–52). This motif was surrounded by POST 5 & 100 PROAVOS INVICTA MANAET HAEC ("After 105 ancestors these remain unconquered"). The reverse had four crowned monograms (IR) in the shape of a saltire cross with an *S* in the centre. Here the legend read DEVS IVDICIVM TVVM REGI DA ("Give the king Thy judgements, O God") from Psalm 72, v. 1.

A two-third-noble was minted in the same series, from 1584 to 1587, and a one-third-noble in 1584. Both were similar to the lion-noble.

LION SHILLING AND SIXPENCE   From 1825 to 1829, Jean Baptiste Merlen's design of a lion standing on a crown appeared on the reverses of the George IV shillings and sixpences. G. W. de Saulles was responsible for a similar motif on the same

51. Lion Shilling of George IV (reverse)

denominations of Edward VII and George V until 1926, and G.
Kruger Gray for later George V shillings and those of George VI
belonging to the English type. Thus, all the coins in these series
are referred to as lion shillings and sixpences.

LIVRA   The basis of Europe's monetary system from the time
of Charlemagne was the *livra, solidus* (sols) and *denier* (£.s.d.).
Britain was the last country to retain it, but finally changed to
the less complicated decimal currency in 1971.

The system was based on 240 deniers being coined from a
livra, a pound of silver. Thus, a *livra* was a weight and not a coin.
A *solidus* was a twentieth part of a *livra* and therefore equal to
twelve *deniers*. Although it had been a coin in Roman times, the
solidus became a money of account in Europe.

The *denier* was first struck in silver but owing to the rise in the
price of bullion had to be coined from a mixture of silver and
copper and then finally copper. The last coin with the name
denier was issued by Louis XVI of France.

LONG-CROSS PENNY   To prevent the clipping of silver
from the penny, the arms of the cross were extended to the edge

52. Long-Cross Penny (reverse), and × ½

of the coin in 1247, in the reign of Henry III. Another interesting feature of this piece was that the King's name appeared with a number behind, either in Latin or in Roman numerals; TERCI or III. This practice of giving the monarch's name and number lapsed until Henry VII came to the throne three centuries later.

LORRAINE   The Scottish testoons, issued in 1558 and 1559 for Mary and Francis, the Dauphin of France, displayed a lorraine cross (✝) on either side of the crowned FM monogram, and therefore they were known as *lorraines*. When Francis became king in 1560, the crosses were replaced by a crowned fleur-de-lis to the left of the monogram, and a crowned thistle on the right.

LSD (£.s.d.) SYSTEM   See Duodecimal Coins.

LUNDY   Lundy Island in the Bristol Channel was purchased by Martin Coles Harman, an English financier, for £16,000, in 1925. For his private island of just over one thousand acres, Harman had £750 worth of bronze coins struck at the Birmingham mint.

There were two denominations, puffin and half-puffin, after the name of the sea-bird which is present on the island in large numbers. Both obverses showed Harman's portrait facing left with his full name and the date, 1929.

53. One Puffin (obverse and reverse)

On the reverse of the larger coin appeared a puffin standing on a rock with the inscription LUNDY and the value ONE PUFFIN, on the smaller denomination the legend LUNDY HALF PUFFIN and, appropriately enough, the picture of half a puffin – the top half. An edge inscription on both coins read LUNDY LIGHTS AND LEADS, a reference to the island's lighthouse. The two coins were to be the equivalent of the penny and halfpenny on the mainland.

The British Government objected to Harman's tokens and prosecuted him for contravening the Coinage Act of 1870, which stated that it was an offence to issue "a piece of metal as a money token". Harman's defence was that Lundy was an independent island outside the jurisdiction of the Crown and that he was therefore entitled to issue his own coinage. The court disagreed, maintaining that Lundy still belonged to the United Kingdom, and it fined the self-styled sovereign £5.

See also MINTS under CIVIL WAR MINTS.

LUSHBURG   This was a coin similar to the English penny and was imported illegally into Britain from Luxembourg and other European countries in the fourteenth century. Other forms of the name were *lushborrow, lussheburghe* and *lusshebourne*.

M

MAG. BRI., MAG. BR., MAG. BRIT., M.B. Any of these abbreviations, together with the word REX appeared on British coins from James I to George III. The title in full was MAGNAE BRITANNIAE REX, (Latin for King of Great Britain), and replaced the ANG. SCO. on the first coinage of James I. MAGNAE BRITANNIAE made way for BRITANNIARUM (see BRITT.) in 1816.

MALTRAVERS FARTHING In 1634 Lord Maltravers bought the Duchess of Richmond's royal licence to mint farthings. He retained the same design for his coins, except for extending the King's name from CARO to CAROLVS. In 1644 an Act of Parliament prohibited the production of the Maltravers and the later type of rose farthings (*q.v.*), but the subsequent shortage of small change was only satisfied with the issue of regal copper coins in 1672.

MAN, ISLE OF The ancient, independent Viking kingdom of Man was claimed by Norway and Scotland before it finally came under the English crown. In 1406 Henry IV presented the island to Sir John Stanley, and he and his successors, the Earls of Derby, ruled as Kings, and later as Lords of Man until 1736, when it passed to James Murray, the Duke of Atholl. Part of the island was sold to the British Government in 1765, and the rest in 1809.

54. Isle of Man Penny of 1733 (obverse and reverse)

Until the beginning of the eighteenth century the islanders used English, Irish and Scottish money, but in 1709 there was a

Manx issue, consisting of cast pennies and halfpennies. The obverses bore the Stanley family crest of an eagle and child over a cap of maintenance, and the motto SANS CHANGER ("Without change"). The reverses had the *triskeles*, or three legs of Man, surrounded by the legend QVOCVNQVE GESSERIS STABIT ("Wherever you place it, it will stand"). The same denominations were minted in 1733 and they differed only slightly from the first issues. The designs were clearer because the coins were struck rather than cast. The GESSERIS in the reverse legend was replaced by IECERIS and the inscription came to mean "wherever you throw it, it will stand".

The 1758 coins of Man were issued while the island was the property of the Duke of Atholl, and the obverse design was changed to a ducal coronet above AD, the new owner's monogram. The first Manx-British coins were copper pennies and halfpennies first introduced in 1786, eleven years before an equivalent issue on the mainland. The Manx coins carried the portrait of George III, as did the 1798 and 1813 issues, which resembled the British 'cartwheels' (*q.v.*) of 1797 and which included the only cartwheel-type halfpennies from Matthew Boulton's Birmingham Mint that got beyond the pattern stage. A Victorian issue of pennies, halfpennies and, for the first time, farthings, appeared in 1839. This was also the year when the Manx penny received parity with its British counterpart, for previously fourteen had been needed to equal a shilling. However, the following year Manx coins were demonetized and replaced by British currency.

No more coins were specifically issued for the Isle of Man until 1965, when a set of gold coins was struck to commemorate the island's two hundred years under the British crown. The five pounds, sovereign and half-sovereign, like all subsequent issues, had Arnold Machin's portrait of Queen Elizabeth II on the obverse. The reverse retained the *triskeles* with its motto, similar to all the types until 1839. However, this reverse was replaced by a picture of a Manx cat on the next issue, the 1970 commemorative crown.

In 1971 the Isle of Man, like the other islands of Jersey and Guernsey, received its own set of decimal coins struck to the same standards of weight, size and alloy as the British pieces. The reverses of the Manx coins were the work of Christopher Ironside, who was responsible for the cat on the 1970 crown.

Each denomination featured a different design which reflected some aspect of Manx culture. The fifty new pence had a Viking ship; the ten new pence the *triskeles*; the five new pence the Tower of Refuge, which was built on Conistor Rocks in Douglas Bay to offer shelter to the ships that were in danger of being wrecked in storms. The two new pence showed two falcons, the traditional gift of the lords of Man to the British sovereign at his coronation. An ancient Norse ring chain pattern appeared on the one new penny, and the ragwort or cushap, the island's national flower, appeared on the new halfpenny.

In 1976 the design of the Isle of Man's coinage was changed, with the most significant feature of the latest coins being the omission of the word NEW in the value on the reverse. The obverses still retained the Arnold Machin portrait of Elizabeth II, but most reverses were given a completely new design, each one being superimposed on a raised outline map of the island. The fifty and ten penny coins kept their previous motifs, but in a slightly modified form. The five pence showed the huge Laxey wheel, which was used for pumping water from one of the island's lead mines. The two pence had a shearwater; the one penny the unique Loughton sheep with four horns; and the half, a herring.

In 1977 the Isle of Man, in common with many other countries, showed her support for the Food and Agriculture Organization of the United Nations and minted the halfpenny with the additional legend F.A.O. FOOD FOR ALL. The intention of the FAO was to encourage increased food production and to use coins as a means to convey their message to as many people throughout the world as possible.

The regular issues of the Isle of Man were minted with a privy mark on the reverse of each denomination in 1979. The privy mark, a stylized trekilion in a circle, was the first to be used on modern coins of the British Isles and was intended to honour the 1000th anniversary of parliament on the island. The following year the design on each coin was changed again, this time to commemorate "the year of the Vikings" or a thousand years of Norse culture on the Isle of Man. The fifty pence had Norse motifs encircling a Viking longship and on the smaller denominations similar designs were incorporated with examples of Manx fauna that had been seen on earlier issues: a peregrine falcon on the ten pence; the four-horned Loughton sheep on the five pence; the chough on the two pence; the Manx cat on the penny and a herring on the halfpenny.

1982 saw the introduction of a twenty pence coin, the first in the British Isles. This was seven-sided like the fifty pence but much smaller. The obverse showed a portrait of Queen Elizabeth II like the other denominations and the reverse also retained the current Norse flavour by depicting a montage of Viking arms and armour.

The original decimal coins were struck by the Royal Mint as was the twenty-five pence struck in 1972 to commemorate the silver wedding of Queen Elizabeth II and the Duke of Edinburgh. Subsequently the contract to supply the island with legal tender coinage passed to the Pobjoy Mint (see MINTS), whose PM mint mark can be seen below the bust of the queen on the obverse of the coins.

Ever since the Isle of Man has exercised control over its coinage, it has taken the lead in numismatic innovation. The use of the privy mark and the twenty pence piece bear witness to this but perhaps of more importance was the issue of the first pound coin in 1978. The "round pound", as it is often called, was the same diameter and thickness as a sovereign with alternating smooth and grained edge sections. This unusual edge prevented blind people from confusing the coin with any other denomination of less value. Another feature of the pound was that it was struck in virenium alloy which gave it a yellowish appearance easily distinguishable from other cupro-nickel coins. The design of the pound consisted of the bust of the Queen on the obverse and the trekilion superimposed on an outline map of the Isle of Man on the reverse. Since the introduction of the pound there have been a number of types commemorating different events not necessarily linked with the island: Henley Regatta in 1979; the TT motor-cycle race, the Daily Mail Ideal Home Exhibition in London and in Manchester in 1980. Each commemorative and non-commemorative issue has also had a security die-mark, e.g. AA, AB etc.

Inflation has shown that the pound is a coin of the future and the idea has been copied by the rest of the British Isles. In 1981, however, the Isle of Man went one step further by minting a five-pound coin uniform in design and metal composition with the pound.

The Isle of Man has also been at the forefront with commemorative coins. The main medium has been the crown, the name which has appeared on almost every issue of twenty-five pence coins. The crown has appeared at regular intervals celebrating numerous events, such as the centenary of horse-drawn trams on the Isle of Man and the bicentenary of American Independence in 1976, the tercentenary of Manx coinage in 1979, the Derby horse race in 1980. There have been others and since 1979 sets of crowns, for example five for the millenium of the Tynwald in 1979 and four for the Year of the Disabled in 1981. The most unusual crown was the one issued in 1979 for the Silver Jubilee Appeal of Queen Elizabeth II. Although part of the proceeds from other commemorative coins of the world have been donated to charity before, this was the first time that a coin had been struck specifically for an appeal. It was issued above its face value and the difference between that and its face value went to the jubilee fund.

The fifty pence has also been used for commemorative purposes. 1979 saw the celebration of the visit of Queen Elizabeth II to the Tynwald, 1980 a Christmas scene and 1981 the TT motorcycle race.

In addition to commemorative crowns and fifty pence pieces, there have been gold issues of five pounds, two pounds, sovereign and half-sovereign in most years since 1973. Each denomination has had a common design, the obverse a portrait of the Queen and the reverse an armed Viking on horseback with his sword drawn. The 1979 issue was interesting in that it had a countermark on the reverse which showed a full-face portrait of Queen Elizabeth the Queen Mother and was thus an extra tribute to her eightieth birthday. The 1981 gold issue had a completely different design with a portrait of Prince Charles and Lady Diana Spencer with the shields of both families below.

The recurring feature of Manx coins is the *triskeles* which has been depicted on at least one regular denomination, and on most commemorative issues it has formed part of the reverse border together with a Celtic chain. The *triskeles* or *triskelion* is defined as "a symbolic figure of three legs radiating from a common centre". On the Manx version the legs are booted and spurred, as well as being bent at the knee as though running. The device goes back to the Athenian coins of the sixth century B.C. and later it reached the Greek colonies in Sicily. Alexander III, King of Scotland and

King of Man from 1266, whose wife's sister was Queen of Sicily, introduced the motif as the island's emblem and it has been retained ever since.

55. Isle of Man Crown of 1970 (obverse and reverse)

MARK A money of account. See MERK.

MAUNDY MONEY Maundy Thursday is the day before Good Friday and commemorates Christ washing His disciples' feet before the feast of the Last Supper, and His giving them a *mandatum* (hence *Dei Mandati*, the Day of the Mandate, and the word *Maundy*) to follow His example.

The first record of an English monarch attending a Maundy ceremony was in 1213, when King John distributed silver pennies among thirteen poor men at Rochester.

The purpose of the ceremony on Maundy Thursday is that it is to resemble Christ's act of humility. The monarch, or nobleman shows pity in distributing gifts of money to some poor and aged people. Part of the original ceremony was the washing of the recipients' feet, but this was discontinued at the time of the plagues in the seventeenth century and the last record of this humble action being performed by an English sovereign was in 1698 during the reign of William III.

A certain amount of food, clothing and money used to be given to the recipients. With the agreement of William IV in 1837, a money allowance was made instead of a gift of provisions, for it was found that many sold the food they had received, sometimes at very low prices. Originally, the sovereign donated some of his clothes to the people. Later this became a present of wool and cloth but it was not until 1883 that money permanently replaced material, after it was finally realized that most of the recipients could not afford to get it made up into clothes.

The Maundy recipients, who must be at least sixty-five years old, are chosen in recognition of a long and useful life. Preference is given to those of good character who have been active volunteer workers for their church or community and who now may be experiencing hardship. The prospective recipients are recommended to the Royal Almonry from the area in which the service is to take place. In the past this was usually London, as the ceremony was held in Westminster Abbey, but in recent years Queen Elizabeth II has distributed the Maundy in churches outside the capital. At the very first Maundy ceremonies in this country the custom was that thirteen recipients took part. Henry IV changed the number to as many men and women as the monarch has years. Thus, when the present Queen was forty years old, forty men and forty women received the Maundy.

During the service, the sovereign or the person who deputizes for him is protected by Yeomen of the Guard and officers called 'wandsmen', who ensure that the ceremony runs smoothly. The Lord High Almoner must also be present. In fact, this officer distributed the Maundy for over two hundred years from 1698 to 1932, when King George V attended in person to perform the task. Since then, some member of the Royal Family has been present each year.

Two distributions are made during the service. In the first, the women receive £1.75p. in green purses; the men receive £2.25p. in white purses with green thongs. This money is in lieu of clothing, in the form of notes and ordinary currency. In the second distribution both men and women are given £2.50p. in red purses with white thongs, and this represents the old allowance of provisions. At the same time, they receive the Maundy money in white purses with red thongs. Formerly, the purses were made by hand out of sheep or goat's skin, but now, of course, they are machine-sewn.

All the purses are distributed from a silver-gilt dish measuring over two feet in diameter and weighing over twelve pounds. It dates back to Charles II, although it bears the cipher of William and Mary. During the rest of the year it is kept with the other articles of the royal regalia in the Tower of London.

Originally, Maundy money was normal everyday currency and the amount required for the ceremony was put aside. The coins consisted of silver pennies until the introduction of milled coinage in 1662, when four denominations – 4d., 3d., 2d., and 1d., (now 4p. 3p. 2p. and 1p., with a rise in value of 240 per cent) were minted. The issues were not dated until 1668 and the first complete, dated set of four coins appeared two years later.

Opinions differ on whether these four coins were minted especially for the Maundy or for regular currency. Some experts consider that only pennies were used until the 1780s. However, one can safely say that the four denominations were used only for the Maundy from 1822, when each coin was issued yearly in as equal proportion as possible, and when copper coins were the accepted medium for small change. Until 1909 the number of Maundy sets was unlimited, and they were available to collectors and the general public through the banks. However, on complaints from the recipients, the sets were restricted to about one thousand, although the number distributed to the poor increases as the years pass because of the monarch's age. They now only go to the recipients and the officials taking part. High prices are paid by collectors for complete Maundy sets when they come on to the market. Odd coins only appear in those years when the sovereign's age is not a multiple of ten, which is the number of pence in a set.

The present Maundy coins, which have plain edges, are the only ones still minted in fine silver. After 1920 all silver coins, including the Maundy pieces, were debased by 50 per cent. When silver was omitted from everyday coins in 1947, it was decided to mint the Maundy in the old standard of fine silver (.925).

Between 1854 and 1927, the threepence is rarely found in proof condition, the reason being that many recipients spent them, as they were identical to the ordinary threepence in circulation. Theoretically they could have done the same with the other denominations as all the Maundy coins from 1816 are legal tender. Under the decimal system Maundy coins have remained unchanged, for no denomination appears on them, only the numerical value. Naturally, very few Maundy coins have ever come into circulation because they are so highly prized by the donees and can command a great price among collectors, once they are able to obtain them. *See* frontispiece for Maundy illustration.

MERK The merk and the double merk first circulated from

1578 to 1580, in the reign of James VI of Scotland, and were valued at 13s. 4d. (66½p.) and £1. 6s. 8d. (£1.33p.) respectively. Both were struck in silver eleven twelfths fine and the larger piece weighed a little under 343 grains. The obverses of both denominations showed the royal arms crowned with the King's titles, IACOBVS 6 DEI GRATIA REX SCOTORVM and the reverses a thistle with the letters I and R on either side, surrounded by NEMO IMPVNE ME LACESSET ("No one will provoke me with impunity"). The reverse designs gave rise to a second name for each piece – thistle and half thistle dollar.

Charles II issued the same denominations, together with a four merks and a half-merk from 1664 to 1675. The designs of all four coins were similar, showing the laureate bust of the King on the obverse, and cruciform shields with crowned interlinked C's in the angles and the value in Roman and Arabic numerals in the centre on the reverse, *e.g.*, LIII/4 (53s. 4d. – £2.66½p.) for the four merks.

56. Thistle Dollar (obverse and reverse)

The Scottish name *merk* is derived from the mark, which never appeared as a coin in England but was frequently used as a money of account. The value of the mark was fixed at 13s. 4d. (66½p.), and the half-mark at 6s. 8d. (33½p.), which were useful fractions of a pound, being two thirds and one third respectively of England's main currency unit.

See also HALF MERK.

METAL SOURCE MARKS   See under individual headings: SSC, WCC, EIC, ROSES, PLUMES, ROSES AND PLUMES, ELEPHANT, ELEPHANT AND CASTLE, LIMA and VIGO.

MILITARY GUINEA   The guinea was issued regularly from 1663 to 1799, but during the Napoleonic Wars it was too much of a risk to import gold bullion from abroad and, apart from the production of the half- and third-guineas, minting of gold coins ceased. To improve the situation, the government allowed the introduction of paper currency. However, there was, in 1813, a final and special issue of guineas to pay the Duke of Wellington's troops in the Peninsula War. This last guinea, with a reverse of a shield of the royal arms within the Garter, is generally known as the Peninsula or Military guinea.

MILLED COINAGE   *Milled* denotes coins struck on presses driven by a mill, so the term refers to any coinage produced by machines, as opposed to hammered coinage (*q.v.*), which was struck by hand. The first attempt at a milled coinage in England was made by Eloye Mestrelle from 1561 to 1571, but, fearing unemployment, the mint workers opposed the introduction of machinery and the Frenchman was later dismissed.

In 1625 another Frenchman, Nicholas Briot of the Paris Mint, was invited to bring his machinery to England, but it was not until 1662 that the rolling mill and the screw press were installed in the Royal Mint on a permanent basis, this time by Pierre Blondeau. After this date, the machine process replaced the hammered method.

Scotland's first milled coin was the testoon produced in 1553 in the reign of Mary, eight years before Mestrelle's issue in England.

MILLING   See GRAINING.

MINT MARK   A private or 'privy' mark of a moneyer or mint was a device by which an issue of coins could be related to a certain period or place, for example, at the request of the Pyx (*q.v.*), which tested pieces for purity and weight. These mint marks were not regularly used until the thirteenth and fourteenth centuries. They consisted of some differences in the detail on a coin, e.g., stops, initials, and variations in the legend and design. At first, the cross, in a number of different forms, was a common mint mark. Later, other signs and emblems appeared, until the last issues of hammered coins in 1662, by which time well over a hundred different types had been in use. In the absence of numerical dates on coins, numismatists find mint marks invaluable in trying to ascribe a piece to a particular mint or period.

In the reign of William III, provincial mints were opened to speed up the recoinage of 1696. Silver coins minted in Bristol, Chester, Exeter, Norwich and York bore the mint marks B, C, E, N, Y or *y* respectively, while those struck at the Tower Mint in London remained without an initial.

In the last quarter of the nineteenth century the Royal Mint opened branches in the colonies to reduce the expenses of striking the locally mined gold and to cut transport costs to a minimum. These colonial mints produced gold sovereigns and half-sovereigns for circulation in Britain alongside Royal Mint coins from 1871 to 1932.

The mint marks were as follows: M, Melbourne (1872–1931); S, Sydney (1871–1926); P, Perth (1899–1931); I, Bombay (1918, sovereigns only); SA, Pretoria (1923–32); C, Ottawa (1908–19, sovereigns only). See also H and KN.

MINTS   There were a great many towns in Anglo-Saxon England which possessed mints, and their names, and in many cases that of the moneyer, appeared on the coins of the period. Prior to the Norman Conquest there were as many as eighty-seven different mints, including the ecclesiastical ones (chiefly Canterbury, York, Durham and London), but the new rulers did little at first to change this state of affairs and it took almost two centuries for the number to be reduced considerably. The process of centralization was not completed until late in the Tudor period, when all but the Tower Mint were closed. The history of the Scottish mints is very similar, the number being decreased until the reign of James VI, when only Edinburgh was still open. After the union of England and Scotland under the same king, both capitals produced coins for their respective countries until 1709, when the Edinburgh mint was closed.

The Civil War, however, had seen the opening of several provincial mints. Parliamentarian forces seized the Tower Mint in 1642, after Charles I's escape from the capital. In 1637 a mint had opened at Aberystwyth to coin silver from the Welsh mines; it was closed in 1642. In the same year, Charles set up his first mint at York and later one at Shrewsbury. When he moved his headquarters from Shrewsbury to Oxford in 1642, the king took his mint with him, but on the capture of the city by Cromwell in 1646 production there ceased and moved to another centre. Other mints during the Civil War period were: Appledore, Barnstaple, Bideford or Lundy Island (1645–6); Bristol (1643–5); Chester (1644); Exeter (1643–6); Salisbury or Sandsfoot Castle (1644); Truro (1642–3); Weymouth (1643–4); Worcester (1646); York (1642–4).

Oxford was Charles's chief mint, but as his armies were scattered throughout the country, centralization was impossible, hence the establishment of these other mints in Royalist strongholds, which closed and moved to the next place when the towns seemed likely to fall to the Parliamentarians.

Provincial mints were also opened for a short time during the reign of William III, but this time they were to help the Tower Mint replace all the hammered silver still circulating, with milled coins as quickly as possible. Mints were open from 1696 to 1697 in Bristol, Chester, Exeter, Norwich and York and the silver struck there bore the mint marks, B, C, E, N, Y or *y* respectively.

Since the closing of the Edinburgh mint in 1709, British coins were minted in London, in the Tower until 1816 and then in the larger building on Tower Hill. In the period after the Second World War it was recognized that even bigger premises were needed for the production of coin for the home and foreign markets, and the Royal Mint moved to a site at Llantrisant in South Wales in 1970, with the Tower Hill centre remaining open to undertake more specialized work.

Since 1709, coins minted at places other than the Royal Mint's main factory include the gold sovereigns and half-sovereigns struck at the branch mints in the colonies from 1871 to 1932 (see MINT MARKS), copper pennies and twopences at Boulton and Watt's Soho Mint in Birmingham, and bronze pieces at other private Birmingham mints at times between 1874 and 1919 when the demands on the Royal Mint were too great.

Birmingham has featured rather prominently in the production of coins and minting machinery in the last two centuries. Her rise to importance as the largest provincial mint since the Industrial Revolution began in the eighteenth century when the city was a centre for the counterfeit trade in coins. The metalworking firms there had all the necessary equipment to produce them and later they manufactured tokens, which, due to the lack of small change, had become the currency of the day.

It was Matthew Boulton who made Birmingham a respectable coin-manufacturing city. To answer the counterfeiters, Boulton campaigned for an improved coinage. In addition, he and James Watt installed the latest machines in their Soho foundry at Handsworth, Birmingham, which were able to produce fifty large or one hundred and fifty small coins a minute. Their first contract was to supply coins to the East India Company in 1786 and eleven years later the British Government was persuaded to allow them to mint a British regal issue – the famous 'cartwheel' coins of 1797 (*q.v.*).

After Boulton's death in 1809, the mint declined, and in 1851 it was acquired by Ralph Heaton & Sons, who attempted to build up the business again. Heaton's was a mechanical engineering firm which had begun as a foundry producing brassware. In the same year as the purchase of the Soho foundry, Heaton's received their first coin contract – for the Chilean half and one centavo. In 1853 the firm was requested to supply the British Government with copper coins ranging from pennies to quarter farthings. By 1860 larger premises were found so that the orders from a number of foreign countries could be fulfilled. Heaton's work had the mint mark H (*q.v.*), which last appeared on British coins in 1919. The firm is now known as the Birmingham Mint Ltd, and has a number of subsidiary companies. Apart from being a major supplier of coin blanks and tokens, and minting coins for many overseas countries, some sections of the group specialize in buttons and badges, emblems and nameplates.

The Kings Norton Metal Company Ltd, whose work was identified by the initials KN (*q.v.*), was another famous Birmingham mint. It became prominent after striking a medal commemorating the coronation of King Edward VII and later for two issues of pennies for the Royal Mint for circulation in Britain in 1918 and 1919. The company manufactured a great amount of coins, blanks and tokens for many countries in America, Africa and Asia. It still continues to do so under its new name of the IMI Kynoch Mint, a section of Imperial Metal Industries Ltd, of which the controlling interest belongs to ICI.

The Birmingham Mint and the IMI Kynoch Mint are the largest and possibly the most well known to British people because of the coins minted for the British Isles. However, the city can still boast of many other mints which may be known principally as experts in the field of medals.

In recent years a few private mints in the London area have risen to importance. One is the old firm of John Pinches Medallists Ltd, now a subsidiary of the Franklin Mint of Pennsylvania, U.S.A., the largest private minting organization in the world. Since 1977 the firm's name has been changed to the Franklin Mint Ltd. Another is the recently founded Danbury Mint which specializes in commemorative items.

The south of England-based Pobjoy Mint had its beginnings just before the turn of the century as a manufacturer of gold and jewellery. The manufacture of badges and regalia led to the commemorative medal and later the company decided to branch out into the field of coin production. The first contract for legal tender coinage came from Bolivia and later another was made with Senegal. The Pobjoy Mint has become well known to British people since 1973, when it took over production of Isle of Man currency from the Royal Mint. The firm displays its PM mint mark on the obverse of each Manx coin.

MODEL COINS   The most well-known model coins were produced by Joseph Moore, a Birmingham die-sinker, and Ludwig Christian Lauer, a German engraver from Nuremberg. Moore was active in the middle of the nineteenth century and there is some discussion as to whether his coins were simply toys or a suggestion for an improved coinage. The pieces range from a sixteenth of a farthing to a crown with the halfpenny and penny being the commonest.

Lauer operated later in the century and his coins are minute copies of real coins which were struck as souvenirs or for use in doll's houses. These German-made pieces comprise mainly the denominations of the 'young head' and 'jubilee head' coinage of Victoria, as well as one piece set with the portrait of Edward VII.

MODIFIED EFFIGY   This is the term for the new smaller effigy of George V which appeared regularly on bronze coins from 1928 until the King's death in 1936. A modified effigy penny was struck as early as 1926 in an attempt to eliminate the 'ghosting' effect (*q.v.*) on bronze coins up to that date. As it was successful, it was adopted as the regular portrait after 1927.

MONEY OF NECESSITY   See EMERGENCY MONEY.

N

NEAP. PR. HISP.   These titles appeared in the legend of the early coins of the joint reign of Philip and Mary from 1554 to 1558. They meant that they were also King and Queen of Naples and Prince and Princess of Spain. On the King's return to Spain, both titles were omitted.

NICKNAMES   Throughout the centuries most coins have had nicknames. Very often the derivations are difficult to substantiate and in the search for the origins very tenuous arguments are sometimes put forward. Some nicknames, however, have a historical connection or are local in nature. For others, the names may allude to the colour, size or weight. The following is a selection of nicknames of various denominations since the sixteenth century. Many are no longer in use, especially since the disappearance of gold coins and the introduction of decimal currency. Some names have been popular for long periods, others were fashionable for just a short time.

Money: 'bit', 'bung', 'blunt', 'brass', 'brown' (usually restricted to copper coins), 'darby', 'dibs', 'ducats', 'dust', 'oof', 'ooftish' (from the German *auf Tisch, i.e.,* 'ready money'), 'posh', 'ready', 'scriddick', 'scuddick', 'scuddock', 'scuttick', 'skiddick' and 'scurrick'; 'groceries', 'mopus' and 'rigmarie' (from REG MARIE on legend of base silver coins of Mary I) were usually reserved for coins of small value; 'duffer', 'slip', and 'smasher' for counterfeit pieces; 'pelf' for ill-gotten money; 'flimsy' for paper money.

Gold coins (guinea and sovereign); 'canary', 'cooter', 'couter', 'geordie', 'goldfinch', 'james', 'jim o'goblin' (cockney rhyming slang for sovereign, later abbreviated to 'jimmy'), 'jingle boy', 'marigold', 'meg', 'ned', 'quid', 'ruddock', 'shiner', 'spanker', 'yellow boy'.

Half-Sovereign: 'smelt'.

Crown: 'ball', 'caroon', 'decus' (from the edge lettering DECUS ET TUTAMEN), 'dollar' (association with American dollar which was worth five shillings).

Half-Crown: 'alderman', 'bull', 'half-dollar', 'tosheroon', 'tusseroon' (possibly from the Lingua Franca – the Italian of the Levant without inflexions – *mazda caroon*).

Shilling: 'bob', 'hog', 'stag', 'thirteener' (for the Irish shilling when thirteen Irish pence equalled one shilling).

Sixpence: 'bender', 'fiddler', 'pig', 'simon', 'sprat', 'tizzy', 'tanner'.

Fourpence: 'bit', 'flag', 'joey'.

Threepence: 'thrummer'.

Twopence: 'deuce'.

Halfpenny: 'halfling', 'mag', 'magpie', 'make', 'meke', 'posh', 'tumbling tom'.

Farthing: 'fadge', 'gig', 'jack', 'mite' (more often for a coin of even smaller value), 'rag', 'rap'.

Amounts of higher values have had nicknames, especially in betting circles:

£5 is a 'fiver' or a 'horse',

£10 is a 'tenner',

£25 is a 'pony',

£500 is a 'monkey',

£100,000 is a 'plum'.

NINEPENCE Thomas Wyon, Jr designed a ninepenny bank token which was to be circulated in Britain in 1812 together with the three-shilling and eighteen-pence pieces (*q.v.*). However, the ninepence never got beyond the pattern stage. In design, it was a smaller version of the first issue of the other two coins.

Ninepence was also a denomination in the siege money of Newark and the Inchiquin money of necessity (*q.v.*), both of which were issued during the Civil War.

NOBLE The noble and its fractions superseded the florin, leopard and helm of Edward III's first gold coinage of 1344. The new gold denominations appeared in the same year but no specimens of the half-noble exists today from this issue, the earliest known example being from the second coinage of 1346. The noble and its half both showed the King in a ship holding a sword and a shield with the arms of England and France quartered upon it. This obverse design is generally assumed to be an allusion to Edward's naval victory at Sluys in 1340. In 1344 the king was preparing another invasion of France and wished to show his country's superiority at sea. The quarter-noble was not unlike the helm, with a shield bearing the royal arms of England and France quartered within a *tressure* of arcs. The reverse of all three coins was a cross with lions and crowns between the limbs, all within the *tressure* of arcs. To prevent clipping, the engravers appealed to any religious or superstitious beliefs or a prospective criminal might have, by inscribing a Biblical text on the edge of the reverse: IHC AVTEM TRANSIENS PER MEDIVM ILLORVM IBAT ("But Jesus, passing through the midst of them, went his way") from Luke 4, v. 30, was put on the noble; DOMINE NE IN FVRORE TVO ARGVAS ("Lord, rebuke me not in Thine anger") from Psalm 6, v. 1, on the half noble; and EXALTIBITVR IN GLORIA ("He shall be exalted in glory") from Psalm 112, v. 9, on the quarter-noble. The same texts had appeared on the florin, leopard and helm respectively.

When it was first issued, the noble weighed $136\frac{3}{4}$ grains of gold, 23 carats $3\frac{1}{2}$ grains fine, and its value was fixed at half a mark, 6s. 8d. ($33\frac{1}{2}$p.). (The mark, the equivalent of 13s. 4d. [$66\frac{1}{2}$p.], was a money of account in England.) The rate of the noble was very convenient, for 6s. 8d. was one third of a pound. The noble retained the same value and was struck in gold of the same fineness until shortly before it was abandoned altogether, but it was gradually reduced in weight. After only two years it weighed only $128\frac{1}{2}$ grains, in 1351 it was reduced to 120 grains and in 1412 to 108 grains. It is also significant that its successor, the 'angel' of the second coinage of Edward IV, had only 80 grains of gold when it was first minted in 1465. It was in the same year that the 'noble' coinage was discontinued, for it had been decided to retain the same weight of 108 grains but revalue the noble to the inconvenient amount of 8s. 4d. ($41\frac{1}{2}$p.) which was not a simple fraction of the mark or the pound.

57. Noble of 1344 (obverse and reverse)

In Scotland the first gold noble appeared in 1357, in the reign of David II. It was almost identical to its English counterpart right down to the inscription. The only exceptions were the shield on the obverse, which naturally showed the Scottish royal arms of a lion rampant, and the weight which was only 120 grains. No other nobles were issued in Scotland until the reign of James VI (1567–1625). These went under the names of 'lion noble' and 'thistle noble' (*q.v.*) and then until the reign of Charles II coins issued at the rate of 6s. 8d. were called forty penny pieces or half-merks (*q.v.*)

See also ROSE NOBLE.

NONSUNT   This was another name for the twelve-penny groat (*q.v.*).

NORTHUMBERLAND SHILLING   Except for Maundy money, this coin, which was struck in 1763, was the only silver piece issued during the first part of the reign of George III. The shilling owed its name to the fact that the Duke of Northumberland distributed a small issue of coins of this denomination to the people of Dublin on his appointment as Lord Lieutenant of Ireland that year, and it is believed that they were struck to gain the favour of the Irish. The high price of silver at that time meant that no other silver coins, again with the exception of Maundy money, were struck until 1787.

The Northumberland shilling showed a youthful bust of the King, by Richard Yeo. The reverse, probably the work of the same engraver, had four shields in cruciform with the star of the Order of the Garter in the centre, rather like the later issues except that the spaces between the shield were plain instead of each containing a crown.

NVMMORVM FAMVLVS   This Latin phrase, meaning "a servant of coins", was inscribed round the edge of the tin issues of Charles II, James II and William and Mary.

O

OBOLE   Halfpennies or half-deniers circulated by Henry II for his French possessions were known as oboles, the anglicized form of the Latin, *obolus*, or in plural form, *oboli*.
See ANGLO-GALLIC COINS.

OBOLUS   This was the Latin word for the English halfpenny.

OBSIDIONAL MONEY   See EMERGENCY MONEY and SIEGE HALFPENNY.

OLD HEAD   See VEILED HEAD.

ONE-SHILLING PIECE   See SIXTY-SHILLING PIECE.

ONE NEW PENNY   Together with the two new pence and the half new penny, this bronze decimal coin, a hundredth part of a pound, first appeared on 15th February 1971, when decimal currency was introduced. The obverse showed Arnold Machin's portrait of Elizabeth II, and the reverse the Tudor emblem of a portcullis, by Christopher Ironside. Below this latter design, which is similar to the threepence of the old duodecimal system ($\pounds$.s.d.), there is the figure 1. In 1982 the word 'NEW' was omitted.

ONE-THIRD GROAT   From 1526 to 1539, James V of Scotland issued a groat worth 1s. 6d. ($7\frac{1}{2}$p.) and a smaller silver coin which circulated for 6d. ($2\frac{1}{2}$p.). This second piece was therefore known as the one-third groat. Both coins were similar, showing a profile bust of the King crowned, facing left, on the obverse, and a Scottish shield on a cross on the reverse.

ORMONDE MONEY   James, Marquis of Ormonde commanded the royalist forces in Ireland at the beginning of the Civil War. In 1643, before his appointment as Lord Lieutenant of Ireland, he minted a money of necessity for Charles I. The silver coins which showed the King's monogram crowned on the obverse, and the value in shillings and pence in Roman numerals on the reverse, included the following denominations: crown, half-crown, shilling, sixpence, groat, threepence and twopence.

58. Ormonde Crown (obverse and reverse)

OXFORD CROWN This rarity is greatly prized by collectors and has been sometimes counterfeited by those wishing to make a quick fortune out of the unsuspecting. It was designed for Charles I in 1644 by Thomas Rawlins, one of the chief engravers at the Oxford mint. Following his defeat at Edgehill in 1642, Charles I set up his headquarters in Oxford and remained there for three years. It was from here that most of his coins of this period were minted, from silver donated by royalist supporters.

59. Oxford Crown (obverse and reverse)

The Oxford mint issued three different crowns. Each showed, on the obverse, Charles on horseback with a drawn sword. However, only the last issue is known specifically by the name 'Oxford crown', for a view of the city was engraved below the equestrian figure of the King. The obverse legend read CAROLVS D.G. MAGN: BRIT: FRAN: ET HIBER: REX. On the reverse was the King's declaration, in two lines across the centre with scrolls above and below, RELIG. PROT. LEG. ANG. LIBER. PARL. ("The Protestant religion, the laws of England, the liberties of Parliament"). (See also DECLARATION TYPE). Above the declaration was the value in shillings in Roman numerals and the three plumes of the Oxford mint. Below appeared the date and the word OXON (Oxford). The whole design was within the inscription EXVRGAT DEVS DIS-SIPENTVR INIMICI ("Let God arise, let His enemies be scattered".) from Psalm 68, v. 1.

P

PATRICK   This was the name given to a billon half-farthing struck for use in Ireland early in the reign of Edward IV (1461–83), and stemmed from the word PATRIK on the obverse, which also depicted a branch and a crown. The reverse showed a long cross extending to the rim of the coin. A similar piece was the St Patrick Salvator farthing (*q.v.*).

PATTERN   A coin struck from a design which is not eventually accepted for normal circulation is called a pattern. It is an example of what might have been. A pattern usually has a plain edge. There have been famous patterns in the coinages of the British Isles, *e.g.*, Thomas Simon's Petition Crown and Thomas Rawlins' Oxford Crown (*q.v.*).

See also PROOF.

PENINSULA GUINEA   See MILITARY GUINEA.

PENNY   The English silver penny was introduced in Anglo-Saxon times and replaced the *sceats* and *thrymsas*. Its model was the denier, named after the Roman *denarius* and introduced by Pepin the Short (751–68), the father of Charlemagne. Two hundred and forty deniers or pennies, weighing $22\frac{1}{2}$ grains each, were struck for one pound of silver.

King Heaberht of Kent is now credited with the introduction of the first penny. However, it was Offa (757–96), the King of Mercia and conqueror of Kent, who made the penny popular and continued its production. The pennies of Offa are admired for their high standard of design and workmanship, which remained unsurpassed for centuries. It was not surprising that the striking of pennies spread to other regions and the penny became the accepted unit of currency for the whole of England.

After Offa, the artistic quality of pennies deteriorated as high production was more important because of the *danegeld* which was required in large amounts to pay the Danish invaders. In 1180 Henry II introduced the 'short-cross' penny which lasted for many years. The short cross on the reverse only extended to the inner circle of the design, but in 1247 it was replaced by a long cross reaching to the very edge of the coin, which was an attempt to prevent clipping for if one end of any of the arms of the cross was cut away the coin ceased to be legal tender. This design remained unaltered until 1278 and even then changed very little until the sixteenth century.

60. Penny of William I (obverse and reverse), and ×2

The cross had the second purpose of enabling the coin to be cut into halves and quarters to make halfpennies and farthings, although this practice ceased when round coins of these denominations were introduced late in the thirteenth century in the reign of Edward I. The obverse of the silver penny had almost always a facing crowned portrait of the sovereign.

In the course of time the penny diminished in size and weight so much that it was no longer economic to strike it in silver. In fact, it became associated with Maundy money and small change consisted predominantly of copper or tin halfpennies and farthings. The following table shows how the weight of the penny was reduced since Norman times:

$$1066 - 22\tfrac{1}{2} \text{ grains}$$
$$1279 - 22\tfrac{1}{4}$$
$$1344 - 20\tfrac{1}{4}$$
$$1346 - 20$$
$$1351 - 18$$
$$1412 - 15$$
$$1464 - 12$$
$$1526 - 10\tfrac{3}{4}$$
$$1545 - 10 \text{ (inc. a reduction in fineness)}$$
$$1551 - 8$$
$$1601 - 7\tfrac{3}{4}$$

After the recoinage of 1816, when the silver penny was solely used for Maundy purposes, its weight was cut by another $\tfrac{1}{2}$ grain. It is true that during the Tudor period, Edward VI introduced a penny of $12\tfrac{1}{2}$ grains in 1550, and Mary and Philip and Mary circulated a piece of 12 grains alongside the 8 grain penny, but in both instances each heavier type contained a high amount of alloy, the silver fineness being greatly reduced. It was not until 1601 that the silver in a penny was restored to its original fineness, and this has remained constant ever since, except for the period 1920 to 1947. During this period, Maundy money, including the penny, was struck from a 50 per cent silver alloy, along with all the other silver coins. In 1947, when it was decided to have only a token coinage in base metals, the Maundy pieces were exempt and were once more minted in silver 11 oz. 2 dwt. fine.

In 1797, to combat the widespread circulation of tokens and forgeries, it was at last agreed to strike pennies in base metal. The result was Matthew Boulton's copper 'cartwheel' (*q.v.*). However, this coin soon gave way to a more popular, lighter and less cumbersome copper penny. The first example of a base metal penny seems to be a pattern struck in 1601. This showed the portrait of Elizabeth I with the words THE PLEDGE OF on the obverse. The reverse continued the obverse inscription with A PENNY, which encircled the royal monogram crowned. (See also PLEDGE).

In 1860 copper was superseded by bronze, which became the medium for base metal coins, and the penny was struck on a smaller and lighter flan, half the size of its copper predecessor and weighing $\tfrac{1}{3}$ oz. This was the last major development before decimalization in 1971. Except for proof specimens dated 1970, the last dated penny was 1967 and was the last time in almost two hundred years that Britannia appeared on this denomination. It gave way to the Tudor portcullis design on the new penny, much smaller but worth almost two and a half times as much. The penny was retained during the change-over period and could be used, together with the threepence, in units of sixpence ($2\frac{1}{2}$p.), as neither coin had a direct equivalent in the new money. It was demonetized on 1st September 1971.

See also GOLD PENNY, SOVEREIGN PENNY, BUN PENNY, GHOSTING and ONE NEW PENNY.

PETITION CROWN   Only a few specimens of this pattern crown are known. It was struck in 1663 by Thomas Simon, who was Chief Engraver at the Tower Mint under Cromwell. Simon lost his position to John Roettier who had come to England from Holland at the invitation of Charles II. Roettier, a favourite of the King, had won a contest with Simon to see whose designs would be accepted for the new milled coinage. In a final effort to

61. Petition Crown (obverse and reverse)

persuade the King to reverse his decision, Simon vainly produced a magnificently engraved crown with a laureate draped bust of Charles II on the obverse, and the quarters of the royal arms crowned in cruciform with interlinked Cs in the angles on the reverse. The edge was engraved with the raised inscription bearing Simon's petition: "THOMAS SIMON MOST HVMBLY PRAYS YOVR MAJESTY TO COMPARE THIS, HIS TRIAL PIECE, WITH THE DVTCH, AND IF MORE TRVLY

DRAWN AND EMBOSSED, MORE GRACEFVLLY ORDERED AND MORE ACCVRATELY ENGRAVEN, TO RELIEVE HIM."

His petition being of no avail, Simon was demoted to designing the smaller denominations in the coinage while Roettier was given the task of engraving the gold and larger silver coins. Thomas Simon did retain his title of Chief Engraver until his death in the London plague of 1665.

PISTOLE   William III (William II of Scotland) issued the pistole and its half for use in Scotland in 1701. Weighing 106 and 53 grains respectively, they were current for £12 and £6, the equivalent of twenty and ten shillings in England at the time. These were the only milled gold coins ever struck for Scotland and had a fineness of 22 carats. In design both coins were similar, with a bust of the king on the obverse and the royal arms crowned, flanked by a crowned W and R on the reverse. The sun rising from the sea below the bust on both pieces was the emblem of the Darien Co., which supplied the gold for the issue from Africa.

See also INCHIQUIN MONEY.

PISTRUCCI   Together with Britannia, the most famous motif on a British coin has been St George and the Dragon, a design which first appeared in its new form in 1816 and has often been used on gold pieces and silver crowns ever since. It is for this engraving that the name of Benedetto Pistrucci has earned its important place in numismatic history.

Pistrucci was a gifted artist and engraver who introduced a continental style of design into nineteenth century coinage, but in most respects he followed a career at the Royal Mint which was not particularly successful. His time there spanned a period of almost forty years, during which he frequently quarrelled with his superiors, even with George IV himself, when he refused to copy, for a new coinage, a portrait of the King by another artist. After this difference of opinion Pistrucci was 'relegated' to designing medals.

Pistrucci was born in Rome in 1784 and instead of following his father's advice and taking up a law career, he became apprenticed to a cameo-engraver in his hometown. After working for various engravers and earning a name for himself as an excellent artist, he started his own business at the age of sixteen. After a short stay in Paris he moved to London in 1815. A year later, the Master of the Mint, Wellesley Pole, offered him a post at the Royal Mint and St George and the Dragon was one of a few designs he cut for the recoinage of 1816. He was involved in engraving dies for later issues, but after 1825 was employed solely in the production of medals.

His greatest masterpiece was a medal that never was, the Waterloo Medal, which took from 1817 to 1850 to complete, and then it was never struck as a proper medallion. However, the original dies are still in the possession of the Mint. Pistrucci continued engraving medals right up to his death in 1855.

See also INITIALS.

PLACK This Scottish billon coin was first struck in the reign of James III (1460–88) and thereafter until the Union of Scotland and England in 1603. The first plack weighed $31\frac{1}{2}$ grains of 50 per cent silver alloy and was current for 4d. ($1\frac{1}{2}$p.). In the

62. Plack of James VI (obverse and reverse), and ×2

reign of Mary (1542–67) it was reduced to 29½ grains and by a further 1½ grains by James VI (1567–1603).

Mary's issue contained less than 10 per cent silver and although her son, James, raised the fineness to one quarter, the plack was current for twice the original value, 8d. (3½p.). A half-plack was also struck at certain times.

The obverses of these coins displayed the Scottish shield crowned, and the reverses a cross with a hollow centre containing a cross with crowns or crosses in the angles. The reverse of James VI's issue was different in that it had a crowned thistle.

The name plack is derived from the French *plaque* a disc.

See also SALTIRE PLACK.

PLEDGE   Copper halfpenny and farthing pledges were issued during the reign of Elizabeth I to outlaw unofficial tokens struck by private individuals. The obverses showed a crowned monogram of the Queen and the legend THE PLEDGE OF, and the reverses the value in words surrounding a crowned Tudor rose. The coins were unpopular as they were easy to counterfeit and the profit from one pound weight of copper was 10s. 6d. (52p.), 12s. (60p.) worth of pledges being coined from 1s. 6d. (7½p.) worth of metal. In 1601 a few rare penny pledges were issued. On the Queen's death these copper coins were withdrawn.

PLUMES   The Prince of Wales' plumes were a metal source-mark denoting that the metal for minting the coins came from Wales, from mines leased to Hugh Middleton in 1621. The mark appeared in the angles of the cruciform shields on the reverse of certain silver coins of James I (the final issue), Charles I, Charles II, William III, Anne and George II. Some rare shillings and six-pences of William III, issued in 1700, showed a single plume under the King's bust on the obverse and none on the reverse.

See also ROSE, ROSES AND PLUMES, and QUAKER MONEY.

POLLARD   See CROCARD.

PORTCULLIS MONEY   This money was issued on the authority of the English Government in 1600, to assist the country's merchants trading in the East Indies, who later formed the famous East India Company. It consisted of dollar values to counter the Spanish coins circulating in the orient. The weights and divisions were specifically determined to agree with the Spanish *reale* and its fractions. The name 'portcullis money' stemmed from the main feature of the reverse design, the Tudor badge of a crowned portcullis. The obverses showed a crowned shield of the royal arms.

This currency is only mentioned here as it was England's first attempt at a colonial coinage, at the beginning of her empire building.

Another name for the dollar-size coin was an eight-testerne piece. The fractions of portcullis money were half, quarter and eighth.

PORTRAITURE   On early English coins the portrait hardly changed from monarch to monarch. The improvement in coin portraiture was made by Alexander de Brugsal, who had been appointed chief engraver by Henry VII (1485–1509). This German die-sinker struck a testoon with a truly realistic portrait of the king. It was the first profile attempt of a sovereign's head since the reign of Stephen (1135–54), and soon the profile portrait completely replaced the facing bust. Improvements in the

63. (*top row, left to right*) Testoon of Henry VII (obverse); Shilling of Philip and Mary (obverse): (*bottom row*) Shilling of William and Mary (obverse)

portraiture of Scottish coins were seen about the same time in the reign of James V (1513–42). The portraits of the English and British sovereigns thereafter were likenesses, even if they were flattering at times. One notable exception to the flattery concept was the Pistrucci 'bull head' issue (*q.v.*). The engravers could make the most of their art by taking advantage of the ever-improving methods in die-casting and coin production.

Some of the most interesting examples in coin portraiture are the pieces of the three Marys of England and Scotland. Mary I of England, eldest daughter of Henry VIII, came to the throne in 1553 and married Philip of Spain the following year. During their joint reign, until 1558, they appeared facing each other on the shilling and sixpence. The same arrangement was used on the gold ducat of Mary Stuart of Scotland, who was married to Francis, the Dauphin of France, from 1558 to 1560. The jugate (side by side) busts of Mary II and her husband, William of Orange, graced the obverses of their coins from 1689 until the Queen's death in 1694. The Prince and Princess of Wales were portrayed in the same manner on the reverse of the 1981 crown which commemorated their wedding.

It has been an interesting feature of British coins that the sovereign has strictly adhered to the idea of facing the opposite direction to that of his predecessor since the restoration of the monarchy and the reign of Charles II, who wished to turn his back on the Commonwealth, although in principle the motion began with James I who usually faced right, while Elizabeth I looked to the left. The only exceptions to this rule to date have been the copper and tin issues of Charles II and James II, the proofs and the nickel-brass threepence of Edward VIII (See RARE MODERN COINS) and the 1953 crown of Elizabeth II.

POUND The hammered pound sovereign of $174\frac{1}{2}$ grains of 22 carat gold was worth 20s. (£1), as opposed to the 30s. (£1. 50p.) of the 'fine' sovereign or double noble which was struck in standard gold. This gold pound was issued by Elizabeth I and James I from 1561, although the fractions of the half-pound, crown and half-crown appeared as early as 1558. Each of Elizabeth's denominations showed a profile portrait of the Queen on the obverse, together with the royal arms crowned, separating the monogram E.R. The reverse legend read SCVTVM FIDEI PROTEGET EAM ("The shield of faith shall protect her"). Later the three smaller denominations were struck as milled pieces on machinery which had been installed in the Mint by the Frenchman, Eloye Mestrelle.

The pound sovereign suffered a slight reduction in weight to 172 grains and this was retained for the single issue of James I in 1603, before it was renamed the 'unite' or 'laurel' (*q.v.*). James's coin showed a half length portrait of the King in armour on the obverse, together with the royal arms surrounded by EXVRGAT DEVS ET DISSIPENTVR INIMICI EIVS ("Let God arise and let His enemies be scattered") from Psalm 68, v. 1.

Thomas Bushell, the Master of the Aberystwyth mint, struck a silver pound at Shrewsbury in 1642 when he was ordered by Charles I to transfer his mint to that town. This coin is the highest denomination ever struck in silver and was minted in that metal because of the shortage of gold. It was not as if silver was all that readily available but plate donated to the King's cause by his supporters was the chief source of bullion for Charles' minting requirements. The obverse had the King on horseback with his sword raised, the reverse the declaration RELIG. PROT. LEG. ANG. LIBER. PAR. ("The Protestant religion, the law of England, the liberties of Parliament") in two lines across the centre (see DECLARATION TYPE), with the value in Roman numerals and the mint mark above and the date below. The reverse legend was identical to that on the gold pound sovereign of James I. A similar silver pound was minted at Oxford from 1642 to 1644, when the mint was transferred there from Shrewsbury. In addition, half-pounds were struck at Shrewsbury, Oxford and then at Truro in 1643, the last mentioned being extremely rare, and having the reverse legend of CHRISTO AVSPICE REGNO ("I reign under the auspices of Christ".)

Following the lead of the islands Guernsey, Jersey and Man, the one pound coin is due to be re-introduced to Britain in April 1983. It is the same size and thickness as the sovereign but struck in virenium alloy. The obverse has a portrait of Queen Elizabeth II and the reverse the royal coat of arms and the value while the grained edge displays the inscription DECUS ET TUTAMEN (An ornament and a safeguard). The reverse was designed by Eric Sewell.

See also GUERNSEY, JERSEY and MAN.

PRIVY MARK   See MINT MARK.

PROOF   A proof is a coin struck carefully from a design which is either in use or later used for circulation. It is struck to a high standard of perfection and is easily marred by rough handling, or even fingerprints. Therefore, a proof should remain untouched in its case, or at best gently held in a gloved hand. In contrast to coins issued for general circulation, a proof usually has a plain instead of a grained edge. Proofs have been struck of many coins of the British Isles and because of their almost medallic qualities command a much higher price from collectors than their 'brilliant uncirculated' counterparts.

PROOF SETS   Proof sets of the current British coins have been issued in various reigns with some commemorative purpose in mind, for example a new coinage or the beginning of a reign. Some sets have contained all the current coins, others have excluded the gold and Maundy pieces. The most unusual set is, perhaps, the one of Britain's last duodecimal coins dated 1970, three years (four in the case of the shilling) after the last date used on those for normal circulation and over a year after the half-crown and the halfpenny had been demonetized. Since decimalization, the Royal Mint has struck proof sets for each year, although in some cases certain denominations have not been issued for general circulation.

PROVENANCE MARK   See METAL SOURCE MARK.

PYX   The exact origins of the Trial of the Pyx are unknown but the first recorded trial was held in 1248, during the reign of Henry III, when twelve citizens of London and twelve goldsmiths conferred with law court judges to test the weight, fineness, composition and quality of the coins which were to be circulated. However, this meeting did not become a regular event until the reign of Edward III. It was at this time that a trial took place every three months. For the purposes of the Pyx it is considered that slight variations in a coin's design, *e.g.*, change of letters, abbreviations, number of crosses and pellets, were requested so that a coin could be related to a particular period.

The trial was originally held in the Pyx Chamber in Westminster Abbey, but was moved to the Mint in 1843. In 1870 the venue was changed to the Goldsmiths' Hall, where it is still held.

Early trials were presided over by the Lord Chancellor, Lord Treasurer, the Chancellor of the Exchequer, or even the sovereign if he attended. Since the Coinage Act of 1870 the King's or Queen's Remembrancer has had to preside over officials from the Board of Trade and the Mint, and a number of members of the Worshipful Company of Goldsmiths, who meet annually for the trial. The Pyx itself is a box, now a number of boxes, which contain samples of all coins struck by the Mint. The coins are weighed on extremely accurate balances supplied by the Board of Trade. They are checked for fineness (the metal being compared with pieces from trial plates of gold, silver, copper and nickel). The court only permits a very small margin of error but faults have only rarely been recorded.

The trial begins in February and the verdict, signed by all the members of the court, is usually pronounced in May and later published in the *London Gazette*.

Q

QUAKER MONEY This was a popular term for the Queen Anne silver coins with the 'plume' provenance mark, which indicated the Welsh mines owned by Sir Carberry Price and Sir Humphrey Mackworth where many Quakers worked.

QUARTER-ANGEL See ANGEL.

QUARTER-FARTHING This copper coin was struck for use in Ceylon (now Sri Lanka) from 1839 to 1853 and was the equivalent of half a Singalese *doit* and half an Indian *pie*. There were, in fact, only four dates of issue – 1839, 1851, 1852, 1853.

64. Quarter-Farthing (reverse), and $\times 2\frac{1}{2}$

The obverse for this tiny coin was the same as the one used for the striking of Maundy twopences. The reverse had the value in words crowned and the date below.

QUARTER-GUINEA This fraction of a guinea was only issued twice – in 1718 (George I) and 1762 (George III). In design both coins were smaller versions of the guineas which were struck at the same time; the former with four cruciform shields of the quarters of the royal arms, with sceptres in the angles and the Star of the Order of the Garter in the centre; the latter with a crowned ornate shield. The piece proved unpopular because of its diminutive size, although it had been introduced in an attempt to alleviate some difficulties in trading caused by the lack of silver coins.

QUARTER-UNITE   See BRITAIN CROWN.

QUEEN ANNE FARTHING   Patterns for copper halfpennies and farthings were designed for Queen Anne in 1713, but only the latter were actually struck the following year. The untimely death of the Queen in 1714 meant that the issue remained very small. In Victorian times the Queen Anne farthing became an almost legendary piece, for it was considered that only two or three existed. The coin is indeed scarce but by no means as rare as it was once thought to be.

As with previous regal copper issues, the reverse depicted a seated Britannia facing left, holding a spear and an olive branch. However, since this female figure was said to resemble the Queen, her bare leg of previous issues was decorously covered to the ankle.

R

RARE MODERN COINS   There are few £.s.d. coins of the twentieth century that are rare, the most famous being the 1933 penny. Since there were enough pennies in circulation only a few were struck, mainly for trial purposes. Two are in the Royal Mint museum, one in the British Museum and one under the foundation stone of a building of London University. Two others, with coins of the same year, were under the foundation stones of the Church of St Cross, Middleton, and St Mary's Church, Kirkstall, both in Leeds, West Yorkshire. The one at the first church was stolen by thieves in 1970 and the one at the second was removed by those responsible for the church's affairs, who feared that it might disappear too. It was decided to sell the penny and the rest of the set of coins for that year, and they realized £7,000 at Sotheby's in 1973. In addition to these coins, there are also a few pattern pieces of the 1933 penny. These were thought to be the only specimens, but on 19th March 1969 another 1933 penny came to light, and was auctioned in London for £2,600.

The first nickel-brass threepenny bits were intended for Edward VIII and some were struck with his portrait by T. Humphrey Paget and the thrift plant reverse by Madge Kitchener. It is generally considered that these were trial pieces for experimental purposes in slot machines and a few were not returned to the Royal Mint. These 1937 coins are somewhat unique in another sense, for the King abdicated within the year (1936) and no coins bearing his portrait were issued for general circulation in this country. In 1965 one of these twelve-sided threepenny pieces was sold for over $10,000 in the U.S.A.

Proofs of an Edward VIII coinage do exist. One is in the royal collection, another in the Royal Mint collection and a third owned by a private individual in the U.S.A.

In 1976 a fourth set bought by a London coin dealer was said to be originally the property of the designer, T. Humphrey Paget. This partial set, which has since been broken up, comprised the crown, half-crown, shilling, sixpence, penny and farthing. The obverse of each coin showed Paget's portrait of the King facing left, which was a break with the three-hundred-year old tradition in English regal coinage. Since the time of Charles II, the monarch had faced the opposite direction to his predecessor. Edward VIII decided to ignore this tradition because he considered the features on the left side of his face superior to those on the right. The reverse of the crown had the crowned royal arms with supporters and motto like that of George VI in 1937; the half-crown, the royal standard; the shilling, a seated lion with sword and sceptre like the Scottish shilling of George VI; and the sixpence, six interlinked rings. These silver reverses were the work of Kruger Gray. The penny retained the famous Britannia reverse but the farthing abandoned her in favour of the wren, a design by Wilson Parker which was retained on the same coin of George VI.

In 1945, when it was decided that the silver threepence should be finally demonetized, all the pieces bearing that date were melted down. One avoided this fate and was auctioned in London in 1970. In fact, the dates 1942, 1943 and 1944 were struck primarily for colonial use.

In 1952 a number of half-crowns were minted to test dies. Then, both the dies and the half-crowns were melted down but one managed to 'escape' and was bought by an American collector for £2,500.

The story of the 1954 penny is similar. As enough pennies were in circulation at the time, the trial pieces were melted down. This coin subsequently found its way into an American collection, after £2,500 had been paid for it. It has changed hands a few times since, once for over £25,000.

Among the modern Irish coins, the 1938 penny is unique. Again it was a test piece which escaped the melting pot at the Royal Mint, who struck the coins for the Irish government.

REBEL MONEY   The silver crowns and half-crowns known as 'rebel money' are thought to have been issued by the Confederated Catholics in 1643 during the Irish Rebellion of 1642 to 1649. A cross in a circle was the obverse design, while the reverse, in imitation of Ormonde money (*q.v.*), contained the value in shillings and pence in Roman numerals.

REDDITE CROWNS   A series of pattern crowns that Thomas Simon produced in an attempt to regain his position as Chief Engraver at the Royal Mint in 1663 were termed *reddite*

crowns because of the edge inscription REDDITE QVAE CAE-
SARIS CAESARI & CT. POST ("Render unto Caesar those
which are Caesar's"). Obverse and reverse designs were similar
to the Petition Crown (*q.v.*) and the effect of the coin upon the
King was just as unsuccessful.

REGINA FIDEI   See F.D.

RICHMOND FARTHING   In 1624, upon the death of the
Duke of Lennox, his widow, the Duchess of Richmond, received
his licence to strike farthings. Her coins were the same as those of

65. Richmond Farthing (obverse and reverse), and $\times 2\frac{1}{2}$

her late husband except that CARO (for Charles I) replaced
IACO in the legend.
     Ten years later the licence was sold to Lord Maltravers (*q.v.*).

RIDER   This gold coin, worth 23s. (£1.15p.) and weighing 78½ grains, was first issued, together with a half and quarter rider, in the reign of James III of Scotland, from 1475 to 1483. Its name was derived from the coin's obverse design, which depicted the king in full armour, with his sword drawn, ostensibly charging into battle on his horse. The reverse showed the lion of Scotland in a shield superimposed on a cross. These royal arms were surrounded by the legend SALVVM FAC POPVLVM TVVM DOMINE ("O Lord, save Thy people") from Psalm 28, v. 9.

66. (*top row*) Rider of James III (obverse), and ×2; (*bottom row*) Rider of James VI (obverse)

James VI was the only other Scottish sovereign to issue the rider and half-rider. This was from 1593 to 1601, directly before he also became King of England. This rider weighed the same as its predecessor, but only in 22 carat gold, and its value was increased to £5. The design of the coin had also changed slightly. The horse was galloping but did not appear to have the speed of the charger of James III. On the reverse, the cross was omitted and the inscription surrounding the shield was SPERO MELIORA ("I hope for better things"). Also, by this time the date appeared in the exergue beneath the obverse design.

ROSARY See CROCARD.

ROSE A rose appeared on the sixpences, threepences, three-halfpences, and three-farthings of Elizabeth I, behind the queen's portrait, to distinguish them from the intermediate denominations, *i.e.*, shilling, groat, twopence and penny.

A rose also appeared in angles of the shields or under the portrait on various silver coins from Charles II to George II. Here it was the metal source-mark, denoting that the bullion came from the west of England.

See also PLUMES and ROSES AND PLUMES.

ROSE FARTHING This coin, the last of the semi-regal copper issues before the Civil War of 1642–9, was struck for Lord Maltravers in 1636. It differed from other Maltravers' farthings (*q.v.*) in that a crowned rose replaced the Irish harp on the

67. Rose Farthing (reverse), and ×2½

reverse – hence its name. The size was also different, being thicker and smaller. Some rose farthings had a brass plug through them in an attempt to prevent any possible forgery.

ROSE-NOBLE In 1464 Edward IV decided to abandon the noble, which had recently revalued to the inconvenient amount of 8s. 4d. (41½p.). He therefore introduced the angel at the noble's old rate of 6s.8d. (33½p.), and the rose noble of 120 grains, to be current for 10s. (50p.). This new coin in standard gold was also called 'ryal' after the French *royal* coin. The ryal and its half differed little in design from their noble predecessors except for a rose on the hull of the ship on the obverse, and a Yorkist rose in the centre of a radiate sun on the reverse. The quarter-ryal had the shield of the quarter-noble on the obverse, with a rose above. The reverse was not unlike that on the larger pieces.

The rose noble, or ryal, did not have the lasting popularity of the angel, and was not coined again until 1489 and the reign of Henry VII. On this small issue of ryals, the rose was omitted from the ship's hull, but two pennants, one bearing Henry's initial and the other the Welsh dragon, were in the bow and the stern. On the reverse there was a shield of three fleur-de-lis, the arms of France, on a large Tudor rose.

Two more issues of ryals were made; the first in 1553 for Mary, and the second from 1558 onwards for Elizabeth I. These coins were of the same weight as previous types but the value was increased to 15s. (75p.). Both coins are quite rare. They retained the basic design from previous reigns. The queen stood in the ship, Mary with her shield and sword, Elizabeth with an orb and sceptre. The reverse of each returned to the early design of a radiant sun with a rose in the centre.

ROSE PENNY   This denomination, in debased silver only 3 oz. or $\frac{1}{4}$ fine, but weighing 12 grains as opposed to the 8 grains of the fine silver penny, appeared in the reigns of Edward VI (1547–53) and Mary (1553–8) and was so called because of the motto, ROSA SINE SPINA ("a rose without thorns"), surrounding a double rose on the obverse. The reverse had the royal arms on a cross. Edward VI also struck a rose halfpenny similar to the penny but with only a single rose. In the King's same issue there was also a farthing but this had a portcullis for the obverse design, and a cross with pellets in the angles for the reverse.

ROSE RYAL   The rose ryal, or double ryal, appeared in the reign of James I, from 1604 to 1625, and was at first current for 30s. (£1.50), and then 33s. (£1.65p), when the value of all coins was raised by ten per cent from 1611 to 1619. In the last issue it returned to its old value but its weight was reduced from just over 213 grains of gold to 196$\frac{1}{2}$. Like the sovereign piece, the rose ryal depicted the King enthroned on the obverse, and the reverse

68. Rose Ryal (obverse)

the royal arms on a Tudor rose, hence the name. The reverse inscription was A DOMINO FACTVM EST ISTVD ET EST MIRABILE IN OCVLIS NOSTRIS ("This is the Lord's doing and it is marvellous in our eyes") from Psalm 118, v. 23. On the last and lighter issue the rose disappeared.

ROSES AND PLUMES Roses and plumes appeared alternatively in the angles of the cruciform shields on various silver coins struck in the reigns of Anne, George I and George II, showing that the metal came from Wales and the west of England

69. Shilling of 1718 (reverse) with Roses and Plumes

from the "Company for melting down lead with Pitcoale and Seacoale".

See also ROSE and PLUMES.

ROYAL ARMS The Royal Arms are not the personal arms of the Royal Family but of the monarch of the country, regardless of family connections.

At the end of the twelfth century, Richard I had as his royal arms a red shield with three lions. In 1337 when Edward III declared war on France and called himself the King of that country, the shield was quartered, the English lions holding the top left and bottom right positions and a semee of lilies and parts of others, the arms of France, in the other two. This was the first time royal arms were portrayed on the English coinage, on the leopard of 1344, and since then they have appeared on at least one denomination in each reign.

70a. (*left to right*) Crown of James I (reverse) with Royal Arms; Fifty Shillings (reverse) with Cromwell's version of the Arms of the Commonwealth

Apart from the semee of lilies being altered to three lilies during the reign of Henry IV, and the arms being impaled with those of Spain during the joint reign of Philip and Mary from 1554–58, no change occurred until 1603 and the unification of the kingdoms of England and Scotland. The English royal arms, including the French lilies, were placed in the top left and bottom right-hand corners, the Scottish lion in the top right and the Irish harp in the bottom left. On Scottish coins the Scottish lion appeared in the first and fourth quarters, the English arms in the second.

It is interesting to note that Cromwell, during his time as Protector, changed the heraldic symbols of England and Scotland to their respective flags; France was entirely omitted and the Irish harp was left unchanged. In the centre was the Cromwellian family lion rampant in an escutcheon of pretence.

During the joint reign of William and Mary, and then William

III, the lion of Orange-Nassau also appeared on an escutcheon of pretence in the centre of the shield.

In 1702 in the Act of Union between England and Scotland, the formation was changed again. The English lions and the Scottish lion were impaled (half of each shield side by side) in the first and fourth quarters, the French lilies in the second, and the harp of Ireland retained its position in the third.

In 1714 on the accession of the Hanoverian Elector, George, to the English throne, his arms appeared in the fourth quarter. In 1801 all claims to the French throne were finally dropped and accordingly the lilies were omitted from the royal shield. The English lions were placed in the first and fourth quarters, the Scottish lion and the Irish harp retained their positions, and the arms of Hanover appeared in an escutcheon of pretence ensigned with an electoral bonnet. In 1816 the bonnet became a crown, as the Treaty of Vienna raised the electorate of Hanover to a kingdom.

70b. (*left to right*) Half Crown of 1816–20 (reverse) with Royal Arms; Crown of 1839 (reverse) with Royal Arms

In 1837, when Victoria acceded to the throne, salic law prohibited her retention of the Hanoverian titles. Thus, the escutcheon of pretence was dropped and the arms have remained unchanged to the present day.

RYAL This silver coin, worth 30s. (£1.50p.) and weighing over 471 grains, was struck during the reigns of Mary and James VI of Scotland, together with the two fractions; two-thirds ryal, and one-third ryal. Mary issued these pieces from 1565 to 1567, during her marriage to Henry Darnley and after his death, until her abdication. The very first ryal was withdrawn and the legend

HENRICVS & MARIA was altered to MARIA ET HENRIC, as Darnley was only the Queen's consort and not joint ruler. This first ryal piece had Mary and Darnley face to face with the date below on the obverse, and a crowned shield flanked by thistles on the reverse. Here the inscription read QVOS DEVS CONIVNXIT HOMO NON SEPARET ("Whom God has joined, let no man put asunder"). The second issue, with the more acceptable arrangement of names, had a very different design and is known as the Crookston dollar (*q.v.*). The widowhood issue was the same as the Crookston dollar except for the omission of Darnley's name. The fractions were similar in design.

71. Sword Dollar (reverse)

The name given to the ryals of James VI, which were issued from 1567 to 1571, was the 'sword dollar', since the main motif of the reverse was a crowned upright sword which divided the date, and a hand pointing to the value of 30s. in Roman numerals. The inscription was PRO ME SI MEREOR IN ME ("For me but against me if I deserve"). The obverse had the crowned Scottish shield flanked by the King's monogram, also crowned.

As silver bullion rose sharply in 1578, a revaluation programme was carried out. All ryals, those of Mary and James VI, were bought by the government for 32s.6d. ($£1.67\frac{1}{2}$p.), countermarked with a crowned thistle, and recirculated for 36s. 9d. ($£1.84$p.). The fractional pieces rose by the corresponding amount; the two-thirds ryal from 20s. ($£1$) to 24s.6d. ($£1.22\frac{1}{2}$p.), and the one-third ryal from 10s. (50p.) to 12s. 3d. (61p.).

For the gold English ryal see ROSE-NOBLE.

S

ST ANDREW   See LION.

ST EDMUNDS PENCE   The last King of Anglia was Eadmund, or Edmund, who was killed in A.D. 870 by the Danish invaders for refusing to renounce his Christian faith. Later, converted Danish settlers struck pennies and halfpennies in memory of the martyred king, who had since been canonized. The obverses of the pence had an *A* surrounded by the King's name, the reverses a cross and the name of the moneyer.

ST GEORGE AND DRAGON   Together with Britannia, this is probably the most famous motif to have appeared on English and British coins to date. The engraver was the Italian, Benedetto Pistrucci (*q.v.*), who took as his model the George of the Order of the Garter. The design showing St George seated on a horse, slaying the dragon with a broken lance, first appeared on the 1817 sovereign of George III. The whole motif was enclosed within the Garter with its inscription HONI SOIT QUI MAL Y PENSE. The same design with a slight modification – the broken lance became a sword – was featured on the crown the following year. From 1819 right up to the present day the engraving has appeared on a variety of coins from crowns to five pounds, but the Garter was omitted and later the artist's name, Pistrucci, in the exergue, was abbreviated to B.P.

72. Crown of 1818–20 (reverse) with St George and Dragon

In 1935 Percy Metcalfe engraved a modernistic design of St George and the Dragon for the silver jubilee crown of George V. This time St George, dressed in armour and seated on a wooden-looking horse, met with public disapproval because of the artist's modern approach, in contrast with the classical style of Pistrucci's engraving. Thus, Metcalfe's engraving has never been used again, whereas Pistrucci's has been seen on a crown and all gold pieces since then.

ST PATRICK'S COINAGE   This copper currency, consisting of halfpennies and farthings, circulated in Ireland in the reign of Charles II, but it is not known whether it was legally authorized issue. The obverse of the halfpenny showed St Patrick preaching, and the legend ECCE GREX ("Behold his flock"); the farthing showed the same saint driving reptiles out of Ireland with the inscription QVIESCAT PLEBS ("Let the people be quiet"). Both coins had the same reverse design and

73. St Patrick Halfpenny (obverse and reverse)

legend, namely King David playing the harp, with a crown above, and surrounded by FLOREAT REX ("May the King flourish"). On the introduction of the regal issue in 1680, St Patrick's money was taken out to the American colony of New Jersey by the Irish emigrants and used there as currency.

ST PATRICK SALVATOR   This was a brass farthing struck early in the reign of Edward IV (1461–83) for use in Ireland. The obverse showed the Irish patron saint wearing a bishop's mitre, and the name PATRICVS, and the reverse a long cross, a rose, and a sun in alternate angles with the legend SALVATOR.

SALTIRE PLACK The saltire plack of $23\frac{1}{2}$ grains circulated for 4d. ($1\frac{1}{2}$p.) in 1594, in the reign of James VI of Scotland, and replaced the plack which had been revalued at 8d. ($3\frac{1}{2}$p.). This

74. Saltire Plack (obverse and reverse), and $\times 2\frac{1}{2}$

new coin, containing more base metal than its predecessor – over 95 per cent as opposed to 75 per cent previously – received its name from the two sceptres forming a saltire cross with a thistle superimposed on the obverse.

SCEAT At the end of the seventh century, silver had replaced gold as the main medium of exchange. The coins, known as *sceats*, were small and thick, measuring $\frac{1}{2}$ in. in diameter, and weighing up to 20 grains. Designs were various and showed a number of influences besides Anglo-Saxon. Some were imitations of earlier Roman coins and others of Merovingian deniers from France.

In Northumbria, sceats are generally known as 'stycas'. Possibly owing to the lack of silver in the north, the coins from this region were struck in debased metal and finally were minted in copper. The sceats from the south of England deteriorated in fineness but not to the same degree. At the end of the eighth century the sceat was replaced by the silver penny.

SCEPTRE   See UNITE.

SCOTLAND   The earliest Scottish coins belonged to the reign of David I (1124–53). Previous kings had imported foreign coins. David's issues were similar to those of Stephen, the King of England at the time. The obverses showed a profile portrait of the King crowned with a sceptre and the legend DAVIT REX., the reverses a cross surrounded by the name of the mint and moneyer. When Edward I introduced new silver denominations in England, Alexander III (1249–85) struck halfpennies and farthings, but groats and half-groats did not appear until 1357 in the reign of David II (1329–71), the son of Robert the Bruce.

David II was also the first Scottish monarch to introduce a gold coinage. The noble, the only denomination, imitated its English counterpart (*q.v.*). The King's shield bore the Scottish lion, the first time that the nation's heraldic animal appeared on a coin. Twenty years later, in the reign of Robert III (1390–1406), gold became a regular part of Scotland's coinage. Robert III also struck pennies and halfpennies from debased silver known as *billon*, which was often used for Scottish currency thereafter. Scotland issued a copper coinage in 1466, a century and a half before that metal was considered suitable for English regal coins. North of the border it was known as 'black money', in contrast with the white metal coins made of silver or billon. These coins were farthings but were discontinued the following year. From 1597, in the reign of James VI, copper was used regularly for the low value denominations.

After 1603 when the Scottish King, James VI, acceded to the English throne, the coinages of the two kingdoms were similar, although the Scottish thistle very often appeared on the reverse of the pieces circulated in James's first realm. From 1663 to 1707, the year of the Act of Union, Scotland had a milled coinage for which a full complement of denominations was issued. William II (William III of England) struck copper and silver coins together with two very rare gold pieces – the pistole and half-pistole (*q.v.*). After 1707 no Scottish coins were struck but the Edinburgh mint continued to produce pieces for Great Britain until its closure in 1709.

Although the currencies of England and Scotland were originally equal in value, the Scottish coinage was gradually devalued from the last quarter of the fourteenth century until it was only worth a twelfth of its English counterpart when James VI became James I of England in 1603.

The coinage of Scotland had numerous denominations, particularly in the reign of James VI. (See under individual headings.)

SCOTTISH NOBLE See HALF-MERK and FORTY-PENNY PIECE.

SCOTTISH SHILLING As a compliment to the Scottish ancestry of Queen Elizabeth, the consort of George VI, two separate shillings were issued in 1937; English (*q.v.*) and Scottish. The so-called Scottish shilling, from 1937 to 1951, showed a Scottish lion bearing a sword and sceptre and seated on a crown. On its right was a shield with the cross of St Andrew and on its left a Scottish thistle. Although the type may have been a tribute to the new queen, the design by Kruger Gray had been chosen earlier for the shilling of Edward VIII, which was never issued because of the king's abdication.

75. (*left to right*) Scottish Shilling of George VI (reverse); Scottish Shilling of Elizabeth II (reverse)

The tradition of having two shillings was continued in the reign of Elizabeth II until 1966, the last date the denomination carried (except for those dated 1970 in the Royal Mint proof sets of that year). After 1952 a different design showed the crowned Scottish quarter of the royal arms – a lion rampant.

SHIELDS Apart from the one showing the British flag at Britannia's side, no shield has appeared on any regular issue of copper or bronze coins. However, a shield has been a regular part of the design of silver and gold coins from the time of the gold leopard of Edward III. Most shields have shown the royal arms (*q.v.*) in various forms: on a full shield, oval, flat-topped, plain, decorated, crowned, uncrowned, with or without supporters, in saltire (x-form), in quatrefoil (+-form, cruciform).

Different shields were featured on the coins of the Commonwealth showing the cross of St George of England and the Irish harp on separate shields on the reverse, and the English cross on the obverse ('breeches money'). The halfpenny was only large enough to show the English shield on the obverse and the Irish one on the reverse.

The cross of St George was not used again until the silver threepence of George VI, when it was placed in the middle of a Tudor rose. The Scottish shilling of the same reign depicted the cross of St Andrew on the left side of the lion. The shillings of Elizabeth II showed the difference between the English and Scottish shillings more clearly. From the particular quarters of the royal arms the English shilling displayed the three lions passant guardant and the Scottish one the lion rampant.

After decimalization in 1971 no shield appeared on any denomination until the introduction of the pound coin in 1983.

SHILLING The shilling was a money of account in Anglo-Saxon times but it was not until the arrival of the Norman kings that its value was fixed at 12d. (5p.). In 1504, during the latter part of the reign of Henry VII, it finally became a silver coin of 144 grains, twelve times the weight of the current penny. This coin was known as a 'testoon' (*testa* – head in Italian). This name was quite fitting, for the obverse of the English piece bore a superb profile head of the King, the first realistic portrait of the monarch. The legend was HENRICVS DI GRA REX ANGL Z FR. The reverse resembled the groat of the period, showing the royal arms superimposed on a long cross. Here the legend read POSVI DEVM ADIVTOREM MEVM ("I have made God my helper") from Psalm 54, v. 4. The testoon was not particularly popular for no other issue appeared until 1544 and the third coinage of Henry VIII, when it was struck from only 120 grains of less fine silver.

In the reign of Edward VI (1547–53) the twelve-penny coin became known as a 'shilling', the name it retained throughout the rest of its long history until it was replaced by the five new pence of the decimal coinage in 1968. The last striking was dated 1966, except for those in the Royal Mint proof sets of 1970. Like the other silver denominations, the shilling suffered a gradual reduction in weight and after the recoinage of 1816 it was set at 87 grains. The original fineness of the shilling was restored in the reign of Elizabeth I, and this was maintained until the debasement of 1920 when all silver coins were reduced to 50 per cent fine. From 1947 the shilling was struck in cupro-nickel instead of debased silver.

76. Shilling of 1548 (obverse and reverse)

The first shilling of Edward VI bore the distinction of being the first English coin to display the date. The Roman numerals MDXLVIII, for 1548, appeared in the legend on the reverse.

See also Dorrien and Magens Shilling, English Shilling, Lion Shilling, Northumberland Shilling, Scottish Shilling and Sixty-shilling Piece.

SHORT-CROSS PENNY This term refers to the English silver pennies designed for Henry II, in 1180, by Philip Aimery, a goldsmith from Anjou in France. They were so called because the short-limbed cross, with crosses in the angles made up of four

77. Short Cross Penny (reverse), and ×2

pellets, extended only to an inner circle on the reverse. The
design was continued through the reigns of Richard I, John and
Henry III until 1247 when the last mentioned introduced the
long-cross penny (*q.v.*) in an effort to prevent the clipping of
silver from the edges of the coins.

SIEGE PIECES   Between 1644 and 1649, monies of necessity
were issued at Carlisle, Colchester, Newark, Pontefract and
Scarborough, towns besieged by Cromwell's Commonwealth
troops. The money was requested to pay the royalist soldiers
defending the towns and to enable the traders to carry on their
business. Inadequate minting equipment produced rather crude

78. Newark Half-Crown (obverse and reverse)

coins from silver plate donated by supporters of Charles I, and
many of them bore the hallmark or the design. The Scarborough
siege pieces were irregular in size and the coins were stamped
with the value according to the weight of the metal. Thus, a large
number of denominations were struck ranging from 5s. 8d.

(28p.) to 6d. (2½p.). The other besieged towns produced pieces of specific denominations but their shapes were various; Carlisle having round coins, Newark lozenge-shaped ones and Pontefract octagonal ones. Pontefract issued a gold unite in addition to the silver denominations and Colchester only struck a ten-shilling piece, also in'gold. Most issues bore the inscription OBS (*obsessum* – Latin for 'besieged'), the name of the town and the value.

With the exception of the Newark coins which are scarce, most siege pieces are either rare or extremely rare.

SILVER Silver was always the main metal used for British coins from ancient times. During periods of hardship and financial crisis the metal was debased and mixed with another, usually copper. Then, as the price of bullion rose, the sizes of the coins were reduced until it became almost impossible to mint denominations of a penny and below. Therefore a copper coinage was introduced for these lower values in the seventeenth and eighteenth centuries.

Until 1816 and the great recoinage, British currency was based on a bi-metallic system, in which the weight of the gold and silver coins was interrelated and changed according to the price of bullion. In 1816 silver became a token currency to eliminate the complications of this system, and the coins ceased to contain their intrinsic metal value.

After World War I, all silver coins contained only 50 per cent silver and in 1947, in order that the government could repay loans to the United States, coins for general circulation were made of an alloy of copper and nickel, and silver was reserved for Maundy money which was raised to its former fineness of .925 silver.

Silver is now the term for those coins in circulation which, although they have no bullion content, have a silvery appearance due to the presence of the nickel.

SIXPENCE Edward VI first struck the silver sixpence and threepence in his final coinage from 1550 to 1553. They were respectively a half and quarter of the shilling, which had been introduced at the beginning of the century, and were much more convenient fractions than the groat and half-groat (fourpence and twopence). The obverses showed a head and shoulders portrait of the boy king, crowned and robed, with a rose to the left

and the Roman numerals VI or III to the right. Like the other denominations of the period, the reverses had a shield of the royal
arms superimposed on a cross.

79. Sixpence of 1934 (reverse) with six acorns

The sixpence originally weighed 48 grains, half of the current
shilling. In 1601 Elizabeth I had this weight reduced to $46\frac{1}{4}$
grains, but the silver content was restored to the fineness maintained prior to the economic troubles in the reign of her father,
Henry VIII. No further debasement was made until 1920 when
all silver coins had a fineness fixed at 50 per cent, and then in
1947 all silver content was replaced by cupro-nickel. In the
recoinage of 1816 the weight of the sixpence dropped to $43\frac{1}{2}$
grains but this remained constant until 1967, the final date to
appear on a piece, except for those in the Royal Mint proof sets of
1970. After the introduction of decimal currency, the sixpence
remained legal tender, for it was the most convenient £.s.d. coin
without a decimal equivalent ($2\frac{1}{2}$p.). It gradually disappeared and
was finally demonetized on 30th June, 1980.

SIX-SHILLING PIECE   At the end of the eighteenth century
the Bank of England re-struck Spanish dollars and circulated
them for five shillings (25p.). The shortage of silver coins was
even greater in Ireland and the Bank of Ireland re-minted similar
pieces in 1804 and issued them at a value of six shillings (30p.).
The laureate draped bust of George III was similar to that on the
obverse of the English coin. The reverse had Hibernia seated,
facing left, with a harp at her side and a palm in her right hand.
Around her was the inscription BANK OF IRELAND TOKEN
and the date and value in words in the exergue.

SIXTEEN-SHILLING PIECE   James VI of Scotland issued
this fine silver denomination, together with the fractions; eight,
four and two shillings, in his third coinage of 1581. All the pieces
had a similar design and resembled the two merks and merk of

the previous coinage. The obverse showed a crowned Scottish shield, the reverse a crowned thistle flanked by the King's initials, IR. The reverse legend was NEMO ME IMPVNE LACESSET ("No one shall hurt me with impunity").

SIXTY-SHILLING PIECE This silver coin was issued in 1604 by James I after his accession to the English throne and was intended for use in Scotland. In design it was very similar to the English crown and, as Scottish coins were only worth one twelfth of their English counterparts, it had no more buying power than five shillings (25p.). The design differed from that on the crown in that thistles replaced the English roses, and on later issues the Scottish lion took up its position in the first and fourth quarters of the shield. The legend was QVAE DEVS CONIVNXIT NEMO SEPARET ("What God hath joined together, let no man put asunder") from Matt., Chapter 19, v. 6.

Other denominations in the same series were circulated at thirty, twelve, six, two and one shilling. The first was a smaller version of the sixty-shilling piece. The twelve and six shilling pieces were similar to the English shilling and sixpence, with the King's head crowned and the value in Roman numerals behind on the obverse. The reverses of both coins were like the higher denominations. The two shillings and one shilling were not unlike the English penny and halfpenny, with a crowned thistle on one side and a crowned rose on the other. Around the thistle was TVEATVR VNITA DEVS ("May God protect the united"), and ROSA SINE SPINA ("A rose without thorns") surrounded the rose. Charles I struck the same series for Scotland from 1625 to 1636, and again from 1637 to 1642, but the two smallest denominations were omitted from the latter period.

In 1687 James II re-introduced the sixty shillings with two different denominations to complete the series, namely forty and ten shillings. Each had a laureate draped bust of the King on the reverse. The reverse of the sixty shillings had a crowned shield within the chain of the Order of the Thistle which was omitted from the design on the forty shillings. The smallest piece had the four quarters of the royal shield crowned in quatrefoil with the limbs of a St Andrew's cross in the angles, each one of which was headed by the four national emblems; thistle, rose, harp and lis.

The coinage of William and Mary added the twenty and five shillings to the series. The twenty shillings was like the higher values in design but the five had a reverse of the royal monogram WM crowned. William II (III of England) struck the same pieces although there is some doubt as to the existence of the sixty-shilling piece. The reverse of the ten shillings now resembled the higher denominations and that of the five shillings was altered to a crowned thistle. Before the Act of Union only the ten and five shillings appeared with the bust of Queen Anne. Both coins were similar to those of her predecessor.

SOHO   This mint mark, which first appeared on the 'cart-wheel' pennies of 1797, signified Matthew Boulton's mint in Birmingham where he had set up his presses with James Watt. The Soho mint was sold to Ralph Heaton in 1850.

See also MINTS.

SOLIDUS   A twentieth part of a *Livra* (*q.v.*).

SOVEREIGN   In 1489 Henry VII ordered a sovereign piece to be struck from gold of 23 carats $3\frac{1}{2}$ grains fine. It was England's heaviest gold coin up to that time, weighing 240 grains, twice as much as the ryal (*q.v.*), and it circulated for 20s. (£1). The coin was an imitation of the Dutch *real d'or* which was minted by Emperor Maximilian, the Regent of the Netherlands, for his son

80. Sovereign of Henry VII (obverse and reverse)

Philip the Handsome. The obverse of the English piece showed the King on a throne holding an orb and sceptre surrounded by the titles HENRICVS DEI GRATIA REX ANGLIE ET FRANCIE DNS HIB. The reverse had a shield of the royal arms superimposed on a large Tudor rose. Here the legend read IHC AVTEM TRANSIENS PER MEDIVM ILLORVM IBAT ("But Jesus, passing through the midst of them, went his way") from Luke, Chapter 4, v. 30.

The sovereign remained current at the same value of 20s. (£1), except for one period in the reign of Henry VIII, from 1526 to 1544, when it was raised to 22s. 6d. (112½p.). However, certain reductions were made in the fineness and the weight. The fineness, initially reduced to 23 carats, later fluctuated between 20 and 22 carats. The weight, however, gradually dropped from the original 240 grains to 172, and when the sovereign was finally replaced by the unite in the second coinage of James I in 1604, it weighed only 155 grains. From 1550 Edward VI, and later Mary and Elizabeth, chose to issue a 'fine sovereign' valued at 30s. (£1.50). In contrast to the 'pound sovereign' of 20s. (£1), this coin was struck to the same weight and fineness of the sovereigns of their grandfather Henry VII. The 'fine sovereign' of James I was known as a 'rose ryal' (*q.v.*).

The sovereign pieces of Henry VIII, the 'fine sovereigns' of the rest of the Tudors and the rose ryal of James I retained the original obverse design of the monarch seated in splendour on a throne. The royal arms continued to be placed on the reverse, either as the centre of a rose or crowned with supporters. However, the 'pound sovereign' types had an obverse of a half length or head and shoulders portrait of the monarch. Half-sovereigns were struck at the same time as the larger piece after 1545. These ten-shilling pieces were at first a smaller version of the sovereign, but later the design became a head and shoulders portrait of the monarch on the obverse, and the royal arms crowned on the reverse.

In 1817, the 'pound sovereign' was issued once more. The previous year had seen a great change in the British coinage with gold becoming the only standard of value and silver being legal tender up to a value of 40s. (£2). The new sovereign was smaller and thicker than the guinea of 21s. (£1.05p.) which it replaced. It weighed 123¼ grains of 22 carat gold, as opposed to the 129½ grains of the guinea.

The reverse of the modern sovereign has remained constant except for those of bare-headed George IV, William IV and the early 'young head' of Queen Victoria showing Pistrucci's famous St George and the Dragon. The alternative design was a crowned shield of the royal arms, which was the motif for the half sovereign until the 'veiled head' issues of Queen Victoria. The obverses have always portrayed a bust of the reigning monarch.

When World War I broke out in 1914, a paper currency was introduced and notes of £1 and ten shillings (50p.) replaced the sovereign and its half. Thus, these gold coins gradually disappeared from circulation. At the Royal Mint and branch mints production of the sovereign ceased in 1932, and the half-sovereign in 1926. After 1925 sovereigns were for the use of the Bank of England and not for general circulation.

For commemorative purposes, sovereigns and other gold values appeared in the coronation years of George VI and Elizabeth II. Then the sovereign was re-issued in 1958 and most other years after that in order to prove that the coin was still current, and therefore counterfeits, such as the forgeries which had originated in Italy and Syria, were illegal. These were full weight and were made for use in world trade, especially in those Eastern countries where there is a general distrust of paper money. As the British sovereign is usually valued higher than its bullion content, it was a profitable business for the counterfeiters. The forgeries were good imitations although the details in the design were seldom as sharp as on the genuine pieces.

In addition to the normal issue, proof specimens were struck for sale to the general public in 1979. As they proved so popular the trend was continued in 1980 and subsequent years.

SOVEREIGN TYPE   This term describes any coin which depicts the monarch sitting on a throne. The first English example of this type was struck by Edward the Confessor (1042–66) and it is considered to have been an imitation of the Roman *solidus* of the fourth century. King Edward was seated on a throne holding an orb and sceptre.

SPADE GUINEA   This term refers to the crown's shield – in the shape of the head of a spade or the symbol on a spade playing card – on the reverse of the George III guinea, from 1787 to 1799; and half-guinea, from 1787 to 1800, (excluding 1799 in the case of the latter when it was not minted).

Brass tokens of the same coins were struck for use as card counters, and money in children's games. Many were also holed and used as jewellery. Early issues were good imitations with a fairly accurate portrait. To prevent them being passed off as gold coins, many had scalloped edges and were either larger or smaller than the originals (20mm. for the half-guinea and 25mm. for the guinea). Later spade guinea tokens were pure imitations with legends such as "in memory of the good old days"

81. Spade Guinea (reverse)

and "the olden times". In the latter part of the nineteenth century such tokens were struck again, this time as advertisements for traders, bearing legends of initials and names. Minor differences on all issues show the large number of designs and dies used, as well as the variety of manufacturers who struck them.

SPUR RYAL   This gold coin, worth 15s. (75p.) and thus half the value of the rose ryal (*q.v.*), was issued in the second and third coinages of James I, from 1604 to 1625. The name came from the reverse design which showed a large sun with sixteen

82. Spur Ryal (reverse)

rays and a Tudor rose which resembled the wheel or rowel on a spur. The ends of the rays had crowned lions and fleurs-de-lis alternately. The whole of this motif was within a tressure of arcs,

around which was the legend A DOMINO FACTVM EST
ISTVD ET EST MIRABILE ("This is the Lord's doing and it is
marvellous") from Psalm 118, v. 23. The obverse of the first
issue, from 1604 to 1619, portrayed the King in a ship, holding a
shield with the royal arms. This is reminiscent of the obverses of
the nobles, although the hull of the ship was suitably modernized
with gun ports. This was also the last time that this king-in-ship
type of design appeared on the British coinage for the second
issue of spur ryals had a crowned lion with a sceptre holding the
royal arms.

Like its predecessor, the ryal or half 'fine sovereign', the spur
ryal, was struck in standard gold but was appreciably less in
weight. It weighed only $106\frac{3}{4}$ grains as opposed to the 120 grains
of the ryal. In 1611, during the period of financial crisis, the spur
ryal, like the rest of the coins, was raised 10 per cent in value to
16s. 6d. ($82\frac{1}{2}$p.). The third and last coinage of James I reverted
to the original value of 15s. (75p.) but the weight was reduced to
$98\frac{1}{4}$ grains.

S.S.C.   The South Sea Company, which had been reformed
after its collapse in 1720 and had since traded solely on the west
coast of South America, imported silver to be coined into crowns,

83.   Shilling of 1723 (reverse) with SSC inscription

half-crowns, shillings and sixpences in 1723, in the reign of
George I. To donate the supplier of the bullion, the initials of the
company were placed in the angles of the shields on the reverses
of the coins.

STANDARD GOLD   Standard gold has a fineness of 23
carats and $3\frac{1}{2}$ grains, half a grain less than pure gold of 24 carats.
With the exception of the penny of Henry II, which was struck in
pure gold, all gold coins until the time of Henry VIII were struck
in standard gold in England. After 1526 less fine gold was often

used for coins and after 1649 standard gold and other degrees of purity were completely replaced by crown gold of 22 carats (*q.v.*).

In Scotland, gold for minting purposes was first reduced from standard fineness as early as the reign of James I (1406–37).

STATER   The gold stater and its quarter was probably never minted in Britain at first, but imported from the Continent by the Gaulish tribes who settled here in the first century B.C. Later these peoples began to mint their own coins in Britain and, as time passed, the imitations of the design of Philip of Macedon, with the portrait of Apollo on the obverse and a chariot on the reverse, became cruder as the Celtic influence became stronger. Staters were circulated by various tribes until the country was in the power of the Roman conquerors who struck their own coins.

STERLING   Used in conjunction with the English pound, sterling denotes that the unit is standard, fixed and authorized. The term may have come from Easterlings or Esterlings, a European people, some of whom worked in England supervising the standard of the coinage.

The term *sterling* was also used for the English penny in the thirteenth century, most probably in connection with the Easterlings again. In Scotland too, sterling denoted a penny in the twelfth and thirteenth centuries. Here the derivation is considered to have come from the stars in the angles of the cross on the reverse.

STERLINGUS   See STERLING.

STYCA   See SCEAT.

SUSKIN   This was a counterfeit coin which circulated in Britain in the fifteenth century. The name was probably derived from a diminutive form of the French *sou*.

SWORD AND SCEPTRE PIECE   The last gold coins to be issued by James VI of Scotland before he became King of England were the one and the half sword and sceptre pieces, which circulated for £6 and £3 respectively. Both coins were struck from 1601 to 1604. The larger pieces weighed 78½ grains of gold 22 carats fine. The coin received its name from the reverse design of a sword and sceptre in a saltire cross. Thistles appeared in the

84. Sword and Sceptre Piece (reverse)

two side angles with a crown above and the date below. The reverse inscription was SALVS POPVLI SVPREMA LEX ("The safety of the people is the supreme law").

SWORD DOLLAR   See RYAL.

T

TEALBY TYPE   A hoard of nearly six thousand coins was found at Tealby in Lincolnshire in 1807, and comprised silver pennies of the first coinage of Henry II. They were issued from 1158 to 1180, prior to the introduction of the short-cross penny (*q.v.*) of Philip Aimery. Unfortunately the workmanship on most of the coins is rather poor and many are irregularly shaped. Although the pennies were struck at a number of mints, the design was fairly standard. The obverse showed a crowned facing bust of the King wearing armour and a cloak and holding a sceptre. The reverse had a cross with a small cross in each angle.

TEN NEW PENCE   This equivalent of a florin (*q.v.*) in the old £.s.d. currency was issued together with the five new pence in cupro-nickel in 1968 to introduce the new decimal coinage. During the change-over period, the old and new coins circulated together and the former is gradually disappearing. The obverse showed Arnold Machin's portrait of Elizabeth II, and the reverse, by Christopher Ironside, a crowned lion passant guardant with the figure 10. From 1982 the word 'NEW' was no longer used.

TENPENCE   L. C. Wyon, Chief Engraver at the Mint, designed a silver tenpenny pattern piece in 1867 in another vain attempt to support the introduction of a decimal currency.

The Bank of Ireland issued a silver token for tenpence in 1805, 1806 and 1813. The first two belonged to the same type, with a bust of George III on the obverse and the words BANK/TOKEN/TEN/PENCE/IRISH (date) in six lines on the reverse. The 1813 issue had the new bust of the King as seen on the British coins of the period, and the reverse was also modified with BANK/TOKEN/10 PENCE/IRISH/1813 in five lines within a wreath. The same series had tokens of six shillings, thirty pence and fivepence.

TEN-SHILLING PIECE   This Scottish silver coin of $92\frac{1}{4}$ grains of very fine silver, together with the fractions five-shilling, thirty-penny, and twelve-penny pieces, was issued by James VI fairly regularly from 1593 to 1601. Each denomination had a similar design with a half-length bust of the King in armour facing right on the obverse, and a thistle with three heads, crowned, on the reverse. The legend on the reverse was NEMO ME IMPVNE LACESSET ("No one shall hurt me with impunity").

See also FORTY-SHILLING PIECE and SIXTY-SHILLING PIECE for Scottish ten-shilling coins of other coinages.

TESTER   This was another term for a sixpence, or half a testoon, in Tudor times.

TESTERNE   See PORTCULLIS MONEY.

TESTOON   The testoon, the forerunner of the English shilling (*q.v.*), was a silver coin valued at twelve pence.

In Scotland, various types of testoon were struck during the reign of Mary (1542–67). The very first issues, which appeared in 1553, were valued at 4s. (20p.) and were the first milled coins to be produced in Britain, preceding the appearance of Mestrelle's milled coinage in England by eight years. The first testoon weighed $78\frac{1}{2}$ grains of silver $\frac{11}{12}$ fine. The testoon was revalued at 5s. (25p.) in 1555, although the weight was substantially increased but the fineness was correspondingly reduced to $\frac{3}{4}$. After 1556 all Scottish testoons weighed $94\frac{1}{4}$ grains and the silver content returned to its original fineness. The last issue appeared in 1565.

For a coin of such a short life, the Scottish testoon is rich in variety of design. The first types were struck before Mary's first marriage and later ones appeared during her marriages to the French Dauphin and Henry Darnley, as well as during the period of her widowhood after Francis's death. Similar types of half-testoons were struck at the same time.

In 1578, during the reign of Mary's son, James VI, all silver coins were revalued because of the rise in the price of bullion. Consequently, silver coins, including the testoons and half-testoons of Mary, were called in, countermarked with a crowned thistle and re-issued at the values of 7s. 4d. (39p.) and 3s. 8d. ($18\frac{1}{2}$p.).

THIRD FARTHING   Soon after Malta became a British possession third-farthing coins were specially minted for the island.
An English farthing equalled three Maltese grains; the new coin,
one grain. The coin was first struck in 1827 in the reign of
George IV, then in 1835 by William IV and in 1844 by Victoria.

85. (*top row*) Third Farthing in copper (reverse), and ×2½: (*bottom
    row*) Third Farthing in bronze (reverse), and ×2½

All these issues were in copper and were followed by bronze
strikings in certain years from 1866 to 1885, and then again in 1902
and 1913. The copper issues showed Britannia on the reverse;
the bronze pieces the value in words within a wreath and a crown
at the top.

THIRD GUINEA   This gold coin, weighing 43 grains and
worth 7s. (35p.), was first struck in 1797, at a time when no
silver could be minted because of the shortage of that metal. It
continued to be issued quite regularly, along with other guinea
pieces, until 1813. The reverse deviated from the normal design

86. Third Guinea (reverse), and ×2½

of gold coins in that it only featured a crown instead of a crowned shield of the royal arms. Early issues had the date in the king's titles on the reverse but from 1801 it appeared below the crown.

THIRTY PENCE   In the absence of regal silver, the Bank of Ireland issued a thirty-penny silver token in 1808, in the reign of George III, together with the six shillings, tenpence and five-pence.
    The obverse showed a laureate draped bust of the King with the date below, and the reverse showed Hibernia seated with her harp and a palm branch, as on the six-shilling token (*q.v.*). The legend on the reverse read BANK TOKEN, and in the exergue XXX PENCE IRISH, in two lines.

THIRTY-PENNY PIECE   See Ten-shilling Piece.

THIRTY-SHILLING PIECE   See Forty-shilling Piece, Sixty-shilling Piece and Three-pound Piece.

THISTLE CROWN   The gold four-shilling piece issued by James I from 1604 to 1619 commemorated the union of England and Scotland, in that the obverse had a crowned rose and the reverse a crowned thistle. The name was taken from the reverse design and this was the first time a thistle had appeared as a major motif on a coin struck south of the border. The legend TVEATVR VNITA DEVS ("May God protect the united") encircled the thistle. The thistle crown weighed 31 grains of 22 carat gold and these specifications were maintained when the currency was revalued by 10 per cent in 1611. Consequently the thistle crown became 4s. 4¾d. (approx. 22p.). Since this amount was so inconvenient, the coin was not so readily acceptable to the public, and with the currency reform of 1619 it was abandoned altogether.

87. Thistle Crown (obverse and reverse), and ×2

In Scotland a similar coin was struck at the same time and circulated for 48s. (£2.40p.), for Scottish money was only valued at a twelfth of English currency. This version had a Scottish crown above the rose and the thistle, and the initials I R (*Iacobvs Rex*) were omitted from the field on both the obverse and reverse.

THISTLE DOLLAR   See MERK.

THISTLE MERK   The thistle merk issued by James VI of Scotland from 1601 to 1604 had the appropriate mark value of 13s. 4d. (66½p.). It weighed approximately 105 grains of silver,

$\frac{1}{12}$ fine. The obverse showed a crowned Scottish shield and the reverse, which gave the coin its name, a crowned thistle with large leaves. The legend surrounding this design was REGEM IOVA PROTEGIT ("Jehovah protects the king"). There were various fractions of the thistle merk, each with a similar design; they were the half, quarter and eighth thistle merks.

THISTLE NOBLE   This gold piece was struck by James VI of Scotland in 1588. It had the unusually high value of 146s. 8d. (£7.33½p.) and although it was not extremely heavy, weighing only approximately 118 grains, it was minted in gold of a higher standard of 23⅓ carats. The design was not unlike that on the English rose-noble (*q.v.*). The obverse displayed a ship with a

88. Thistle Noble (obverse and reverse)

large Scottish shield crowned on its hull. A flag on the bow had the initial I for *Iacobvs* and one at the stern had the figure 6. The legend was IACOBVS 6 DEI GRATIA REX SCOTORVM. The reverse showed a thistle plant and two crossed sceptres surrounded by four lions and four crowns. The legend was FLORENT SCEPTRA PIIS REGNA HIIS IOVA DAT NVMERATQVE ("Sceptres flourish with the pious; Jehovah gives them kingdoms and numbers them").

THREE CROWNS MONEY   This was an issue of silver groats, half-groats and pennies for Ireland, and was so called because of the reverse design of three different-sized crowns in column formation with the smallest at the top. The design was used for Richard III, Henry VII and Lambert Simnel, a Yorkist

89. Three Crowns Money (reverse), and ×2

pretender to Henry's throne in 1487. The issues appeared between about 1485 and 1490. The obverse design was a shield of
the royal arms superimposed on a cross.

THREEFARTHINGS This coin was introduced with
another new denomination, the threehalfpence, in the reign of
Elizabeth I. The threefarthings weighed only 6 grains of silver
and was issued fairly regularly from 1561 to 1582. An example
dated 1563 was also included in Eloye Mestrelle's milled coinage.
Both coins, like the other silver issues of the period, showed a
portrait of the Queen on the obverse and the royal arms on the
reverse. There was no value on the sixpence, threepence, threehalfpence and threefarthings, but a rose was engraved behind
the Queen's portrait, and the date appeared above the shield on
the reverse to distinguish them from the other small silver coins —
the shilling, groat, half-groat and penny.

THREEHALFPENCE This silver coin was first issued in the
reign of Elizabeth I, and, apart from being double the weight and
larger in size, was identical to the threefarthings of the time
(*q.v.*).
      The denomination was not struck again until 1834, this time
for the colonies of Ceylon, British Guiana and the British West
Indies, all of which used British currency. In Ceylon it was equal
to an Indian *anna*, and in the last two mentioned colonies it
equalled a Spanish-American quarter-ryal. The coin's design
was similar to the Maundy coinage but with figures 1½ crowned

on the reverse. It was issued each year from 1834 to 1843 and then again in 1860 and 1862. The modern threehalfpence weighed only 10¾ grains as opposed to the 12 grains of the original issue, but was minted in silver of a slightly higher fineness. The early Elizabethan coins were only 11 oz. fine, but in 1601 this was increased to 11 oz. 2 dwt. fine, a standard maintained until 1920.

THREEPENCE   In 1551, when Edward VI attempted to restore the English silver coinage to a fineness comparable to that of his father's first issues, he also struck two new denominations, the sixpence and the threepence, although there seemed little justification for the latter as a new value, considering the presence of the groat and half-groat. However, production of the fourpence and twopence were suspended so that two new coins could be established.

The first threepence resembled the shilling and sixpence in design. The obverse had a crowned facing portrait of the King, with a rose to the left and the value in Roman numerals (III) to the right. The reverse had the shield of the royal arms on a cross.

The threepence originally weighed 24 grains of silver .916 fine. These specifications were retained for the issues of Elizabeth, the next sovereign to strike the denomination. Few threepences were struck during the time of the Stuart kings and after, and it is thought that those that were minted were reserved for the annual Maundy distribution. These coins were struck to a higher standard of fineness (.925) but weighed 23 grains.

After the recoinage of 1816, the threepence was reduced to 21¾ grains and soon afterwards, during the reign of William IV and in the early years of the Victorian period, large mintages were more common but the coins were intended largely for colonial use. The threepence was not issued for general circulation in Great Britain until 1845.

90. (*left to right*) Silver Threepence of George VI (reverse); Nickle-Brass Threepence of George VI (reverse)

Although it still survives in the Maundy money – now as 3p. rather than 3d., the last silver issue for general use was struck in 1945 but was melted down again by the Royal Mint. Those minted in the previous three years were for colonial rather than domestic use.

The disappearance of the silver threepence was caused by the increasing popularity of the twelve-sided nickel-brass piece which had been current since 1937. However, this type, originally with a thrift plant reverse and later that of a Tudor portcullis, was not issued after 1967 and was demonetized, together with the penny, on 1st September 1971, after they had both been used in the changeover to decimal currency in units with a direct equivalent in the new money. Examples of the brass threepence dated 1970 appeared in the Royal Mint proof sets of £.s.d. coins of that year.

THREE-POUND PIECE This gold coin and its half, the thirty-shilling piece, were minted in Scotland from 1555 to 1558, in the reign of Mary. Both were struck in 22 carat gold and the larger piece weighed approximately 118 grains. The obverses of both coins showed a portrait of the Queen facing left, and the reverses the Scottish arms, crowned, with the legend IVSTVS FIDE VIVITA ("A just man lives by faith").

Three-pound pieces issued after the union of England and Scotland are generally referred to as 'sixty-shilling pieces' (*q.v.*).

THREE-SHILLING PIECE This was issued by the Bank of England from 1811 to 1816 to prevent the circulation of other silver tokens which had appeared in great numbers throughout

91. Bank of England Three-Shilling Token (reverse)

the country as a result of a lack of silver coinage. With the introduction of this piece and the eighteen pence (*q.v.*), tokens were
prohibited, although it was itself a token worth only four-fifths
of its intrinsic metal value. The first issue showed a draped bust
of George III in armour on the obverse, and the words BANK
TOKEN 3 SHILL. and the date, within an oak wreath, on the
reverse. The second issue, from 1812 to 1816, depicted a laureate
head of the King and the reverse wreath consisted of oak and
laurel.

In 1642 Charles I struck his last series of silver coins in Scotland. It contained only two coins, the three and the two shillings.
The larger denomination had the crowned royal arms, Scottish
style, on the reverse, whereas the two shillings only featured the
Scottish quartering crowned. The three shillings displayed a
thistle behind the King's head on the obverse; the two, the value
in Roman numerals. Each coin had a different reverse legend.
The higher denomination had SALVS REI PVBLICAE
SVPREMA LEX ("The safety of the state is the supreme law"),
and the lower one IVST (ITIA) THRONVM FIRMAT ("Justice
strengthens the throne").

THRYMSA   A *thrymsa* was originally a Byzantine coin which
appeared in the Roman series from the third century. The design
of a profile portrait on the obverse and a cross on the reverse was
imitated on the Frankish coins, which were in turn copied by the
Anglo-Saxons on their gold coins in the latter part of the sixth
century. As time passed the design deteriorated and the inscription in Latin letters began to be replaced by one in the Runic
alphabet, thus showing the Scandinavian influence on England
before the complete conversion of the land to Christianity. By
A.D. 700 the *thrymsa* was superseded by the silver sceat as a result of the ever-increasing price of gold.

The name *thrymsa* denotes three or a third. The original
thrymsas or *tremisses* of Byzantium and Merovingian France
were one-third of the *solidus* (see LIVRA).

TIN   Poor durability has excluded tin from being used regularly in the production of coins. The only British denominations
to have been struck in that metal were the halfpennies and farthings of Charles II, James II and William and Mary. Apart from
its function of simulating silver, tin was used at this time because

it could be mined locally, whereas copper was much more expensive because it had to be imported. However, tin coins were not only affected by the atmosphere, but were also easy to counterfeit and therefore a plug of copper was put right through the centre of the flan. Tin coins appeared from 1684 to 1692, after which only the more practical copper was used.

TOKENS In contrast to a coin, which is a piece of metal of a certain value, issued by a government to circulate as legal tender, a token is privately struck without royal or parliamentary approval. However, since they are used in the same manner as coins, the public generally accepts them as a form of money, even though they may only be redeemed in goods.

Tokens circulated freely in Britain in certain periods in the seventeenth, eighteenth and nineteenth centuries. Although they were prohibited, some lead and copper tokens valued at a halfpenny and a farthing were struck by tradesmen in the reign of Elizabeth I in the sixteenth century. Over the years silver coins had so diminished in size that those of very low value became minute. In the seventeenth century, the monarch at first refused to strike coins in a base metal, considering that such pieces were unworthy of both his portrait and his approval.

In the early part of the seventeenth century, shopkeepers issued copper tokens to meet the need for small change. Harrington farthings (*q.v.*), privately issued with the sovereign's approval, put a stop to this practice. As the intrinsic metal value of these latter coins was low, thus giving the manufacturers great profits, they were unpopular, and when the patent had passed to various people after Lord Harrington, these copper coins were discontinued by Act of Parliament in 1644.

A few years after this, in 1649, until 1672 and the first regal issue of base metal coins, about ten thousand types of tokens circulated throughout the country. The denominations were mainly penny, halfpenny and farthing.

Tokens of this period usually displayed the issuer's name, trade and place of residence, together with a design struck on a thin copper, brass or sometimes lead flan. The majority were poorly struck on blanks of all shapes and sizes, although round ones were the most common.

Regal coins were then struck in small numbers at various intervals for over a century, but the inadequate supply of small change caused tradesmen to issue their own coins again. These tokens were illegal, but were immediately accepted by the public as a popular local medium of circulation, in preference to the copper coins, so worn that they were barely recognizable, and their numerous counterfeits.

The first tokens of this period were pennies minted for the Pary's Mine Co. in 1787 by Boulton and Watt on their new steam-driven press. This contract ran until 1797 and the regal issue of 'cartwheel' copper coins (*q.v.*).

Tokens of the decade can be divided into several classes. There were the genuine tokens of good weight issued in good faith by merchants and manufacturers. These were redeemable and usually bore the issuer's name and address. The values stamped on the pieces themselves were normally halfpenny, penny and sixpence. Then there were tokens of light weight bearing no name and address and struck for anyone who cared to buy and circulate them. Advertising tokens were also widely circulated. These, issued in good faith, displayed the issuer's name and address, often with a detailed description of his business, thus combining advertising and a means of payment. Manufacturers also produced tokens specifically for sale to collectors. These were struck in small numbers and were often medallic in quality as a result of superior workmanship, in contrast to those pieces for general circulation. In addition, there were token forgeries, the production of which involved less risk for the counterfeiter than if he copied regal issues.

After the appearance of halfpennies in 1807, no more copper coins were struck and Parliament continually ignored the public's demand for small change. Thus, tokens were issued again to satisfy this need. Initially, they appeared in the Midlands in 1811 in order to pay the factory workers. The government unofficially approved their circulation, finding them a useful substitute for a regal coinage and one which spared them the expense of buying copper, which stood at a high price at the time. However, the time came for the prohibition of these tokens when certain issuers refused to redeem them. In 1817, an Act of Parliament declared them illegal. Silver tokens were also produced between 1811 and 1812, again due to the high price of metal, this time bullion, and also to the government's unwillingness to coin at a loss or at a reduced profit.

Apart from those used for advertising purposes, the last real tokens were the Truck tokens for labourers' tallies, which were paid to workers who could only redeem them at shops belonging to their employers (colloquially known as 'tommy shops'). The Truck Act of 1831 declared them illegal.

For the most part, tokens were current in Scotland and Ireland at the same time and on the same basis as in England. However, they circulated in Ireland for longer and more frequent periods, mainly because the country suffered an even greater lack of regal coinage than England. This is particularly evident in the token issues of the eighteenth century.

TOUCH PIECE   Persons of royal blood were thought to have the mystic power of healing by touch, and demonstrated their gift at ceremonies where sufferers of scrofula or tuberculosis, commonly known as the 'king's evil', were presented with coins or medalets to ward off the disease. The custom lasted from the reign of Edward the Confessor to that of Queen Anne, although the latter's predecessor, William III, refused to believe in it. A convenient coin for this purpose was the gold angel, with St Michael slaying the devil on the obverse. When the angel was no longer minted, gold medalets were struck with a similar design of good defeating evil. Touch pieces were treasured by their owners and were often pierced so that they could be hung round the neck. This is the reason why so many angels are found with holes in them.

TRADE DOLLAR   This silver piece was issued from 1895 to 1935 and was intended for trading purposes in the Far East. It was therefore minted chiefly at the Asian branches of the

92. Trade Dollar (obverse and reverse)

Royal Mint in Calcutta and Bombay. The value of the coin appeared in English on the obverse, and in Chinese and Malaysian on the reverse. The obverse design of a standing Britannia, by G. W. de Saulles, was the forerunner of the one on the Edward VII florin.

TREMISSIS   This was another name for the *thrymsa* (*q.v.*), and the model for the Anglo-Saxon *thrymsa* was the Merovingian *tremissis* which must have been used as currency in this country, especially in the south of England, where many have been unearthed in hoards and burial grounds.

TRIPLE UNITE   During the Civil War the gold triple unite, valued at three pounds, was struck for Charles I at Shrewsbury (1642) and Oxford (1642–4). The triple unite from Shrewsbury is now possibly unique and although there are several variations of the same type from Oxford, they are all quite rare. Apart from the distinguishing mint marks, the coins from both mints are very similar. The obverses had a half-length portrait of the King holding a sword in one hand and the olive branch of peace in the other. Similar to other pieces of the same period, the reverses had the 'declaration' of Charles I, surrounded by EXVRGAT DEVS DISSIPENTVR INIMICI ("Let God arise and let His enemies be scattered") from Psalm 68, v. 1.

TURNER   James I first issued this Scottish copper coin in 1597 before he became King of England. It continued to be struck by the British sovereigns for "across the border" until the reign of William III. It was worth twopence, and from the time of Charles I it was also known as a 'bodle' (*q.v.*). The term *turner* was a corruption of the French *gros tournois*.

93. Turner of 1677 (obverse and reverse)

The first turner had a bare-headed bust of the King on the obverse, and three thistle heads on the reverse. After James's accession to the English throne the obverse showed a three-headed thistle and the reverse a crowned Scottish lion rampant.

The penny of the same period is sometimes known as the 'half-turner'.

TURNEY This was an illegal counterfeit coin struck in billon and was an imitation of the French *gros tournois*. It circulated in Britain, mainly Ireland, in the fourteenth century.

TWELVE-PENNY GROAT The name of this Scottish coin is a contradiction, since a groat was a fourpenny piece. It was struck in half silver and half base metal and weighed about 26 grains. The coin was issued in 1558 and 1559, during Mary's marriage to the French Dauphin. The obverse had a crowned

94. Twelve-Penny Groat (obverse and reverse), and ×2

monogram of Francis and Mary between a crowned dolphin and a crowned thistle. The reverse consisted of a rectangle containing the inscription IAM NON SVNT DVO SED VNA CARO ("They are no more two but one flesh") from Matt., Chapter 19, v. 6. Part of this quotation gave rise to the coin's other name of "nonsunt".

TWELVE-PENNY PIECE   See TEN-SHILLING PIECE.

TWELVE-SHILLING PIECE   See SIXTY-SHILLING PIECE.

TWENTY-FIVE NEW PENCE   Since the introduction of decimal currency, the twenty-five new pence has been the natural successor to the crown, being its equivalent in the new monetary system. Gibraltar, which issued commemorative crowns annually in the late 1960s, was the first country to use the new name when the 1971 piece appeared. The following year it was included in the legend of the crown-size pieces of Guernsey and the Isle of Man (without the word *NEW*) as well as those of Gibraltar, but the twenty-five new pence of Great Britain, like many of the coins which preceded it, displayed no value. This first twenty-five pence commemorative marked the silver wedding of Queen Elizabeth II and Prince Philip. Since then a twenty-five pence coin has been issued to commemorate the silver jubilee of Queen Elizabeth II in 1977, the eightieth birthday of Queen Elizabeth the Queen Mother in 1980 and the wedding of Prince Charles and Lady Diana Spencer in 1981.

TWENTY PENCE   Britain's first decimal coin to omit the word NEW was the twenty pence which came into circulation in June 1982. This seven-sided cupro-nickel coin was similar in shape to a fifty pence but smaller and also resembled the 'cartwheels' (*q.v.*) of 1797 with its wide rim and incuse legend. The obverse shows a portrait of Queen Elizabeth II and the reverse a crowned English rose. The design was the work of William Gardner who produced the portcullis reverse for the nickel-brass threepence from 1953 to 1967 (*q.v.*).
See also HALF-MERK.

TWENTY-POUND PIECE   This gold piece, struck by James VI in 1575 and 1576, was the largest denomination issued in

Scotland. It weighed a little more than 471 grains of 22 carat gold. The obverse showed a half-length, crowned figure of the Scottish King holding a sword in his right hand and an olive

95. Twenty-Pound Piece (obverse and reverse)

branch in his left. Below was the appropriate motto IN VTRVNQVE PARATVS, meaning "prepared for either" (*i.e.*, war or peace). The reverse legend expressed the wish "to spare the vanquished and suppress the proud", PARCERE SVBIECTIS & DEBELLARE SVPERBOS, from the sixth book of Vergil's *Aeneid*. This inscription surrounded a crowned Scottish shield.

TWENTY-SHILLING PIECE   This rare Scottish coin was struck in 1543 by Mary, whose monogram appeared crowned on the reverse with the legend ECCE ANCILLA DOMINI ("Behold the handmaid of the Lord") from Luke, Chapter 1, v. 38. The obverse had the crowned Scottish shield. The twenty shillings weighed approximately 44 grains of 22 carat gold.

   See also FORTY-SHILLING PIECE and SIXTY-SHILLING PIECE.

TWENTY-TWO SHILLING PIECE   See FORTY-FOUR SHILLING PIECE.

TWO-GUINEA PIECE   This gold coin was issued regularly with other guinea denominations, from the reign of Charles II to that of George II. The last issue for general circulation was in 1753. There were three two-guinea coins struck for George III in 1768, 1773 and 1777, but these were only pattern pieces. The two-guinea was replaced by the two-pound piece after the re-coinage of 1816.

See also GUINEA.

TWO NEW PENCE This bronze coin appeared on 15th February 1971, on the introduction of decimal currency, to-gether with the one new penny and its half. The obverse portrait of Elizabeth II was designed by Arnold Machin, and the reverse, showing the emblem of the Prince of Wales and the figure 2 below, was by Christopher Ironside. The word 'NEW' was dropped in 1982.

TWOPENCE Also called a 'half groat', the silver twopence was struck at the same time as the second issue of groats in 1351. It still survives as a silver coin in the Maundy money. In 1797 the twopence was minted for the first and only time in copper (see 'cartwheel').

See also BODLE and TURNER for the Scottish twopence.

TWO-POUND PIECE The name *double sovereign* goes back to Tudor times but the term *two pounds* was first used in 1820 for the gold pattern piece and subsequently the coin for general circulation which took the place of the two guineas. The most common occasions for the issue of the two-pound piece have been coronation and jubilee years. The dates are 1823, 1826, 1831, 1887, 1893, 1902, 1911, 1937, 1953 and 1980, with 1823, 1887, 1893 and 1902 being the only years when the coin was also struck for general circulation as opposed to just a proof issue. With the exception of the William IV issue of 1831 which had a draped shield, the reverse of the two-pound piece has always shown Pistrucci's St George and the Dragon. The two-pound piece con-tains $246\frac{1}{2}$ grains of 22 carat gold, exactly twice the weight of the sovereign.

TWO-SHILLING PIECE See SIXTEEN-SHILLING PIECE, SIXTY-SHILLING PIECE, THREE-SHILLING PIECE and FLORIN.

U

UNA AND THE LION   This was the name given to William Wyon's pattern £5 piece which was included in the proof sets of 1839. The reverse depicted Queen Victoria portrayed as Una, the personification of Truth from the *Faerie Queen* by Edmund Spenser. She was shown guiding the British lion with her sceptre. Above the design was the motto DIRIGIT DEUS GRESSUS MEOS ("God guide my footsteps"), and below in the exergue was the date in Roman numerals. The edge bore the

96.   Una and the Lion (obverse and reverse)

usual legend for five-pound pieces, namely, DECVS ET TVTAMEN and ANNO REGNI TERTIO. The obverse portrait of the Queen by Wyon was similar to that on the rest of the 'young head' coinage.

UNICORN   The unicorn, weighing 59 grains of gold only 21 carats fine, was first issued in 1486 by James III of Scotland. Its name stemmed from the obverse design of a crowned unicorn with a shield of the Scottish arms. The reverse consisted of a wavy star with twelve rays superimposed on a cross fleury, all of which was surrounded by EXVRGAT DEVS ET DISSIPENTVR INIMICI ("Let God arise and let His enemies be scattered") from Psalm 68, v. 1. The unicorn, together with the half, was also struck in the reigns of James IV (1488–1513) and James V (1513–42). Each type was similar to the very first issue.

97. Unicorn of James III (obverse and reverse), and ×2

The unicorn circulated for 18s. (80p.) at first, but in the time of James V its value had risen to 20s. (£1), and went up further to 22s. (£1.10p.) in the same reign.

UNITE   The unite was the gold sovereign of 22 carats fine which was struck soon after James I's accession to the throne, until the introduction of a milled coinage in 1663. The name of this denomination was changed from the 'sovereign' because the coin's motto was a direct reference to the union between England and Scotland – FACIAM EOS GENTEM VNAM ("I will make them one nation") from Ezek., Chapter 37, v. 22. Charles I and Charles II preferred the inscription FLORENT CONCORDIA REGNA ("Through concord kingdoms flourish"), while the provincial issues of the Civil War (1642–9) had the legend EXVRGAT DEVS ET INIMICI DISSIPENTVR ("Let God arise and let His enemies be scattered") from Psalm 68, v. 1. The Commonwealth issues (1649–60) were of the 'Breeches money' type (*q.v.*), and the Cromwell patterns of 1656 showed PAX QVAERITVR BELLO ("Peace is sought by war").

98. Unite of James I (obverse and reverse)

The final issue of the unite of James I, from 1619 to 1625, was more commonly called the 'laurel' (*q.v.*), because of the wreath around the King's head. The Commonwealth and Charles II issues of this coin were termed 'broad' (*q.v.*), which described the size of the coin, for the reference to the union was no longer valid as that particular legend had long since disappeared.

The obverse of the first unites showed a half-length portrait of James bearing an orb and sceptre, hence its other name of 'sceptre piece'. The reverse bore the royal arms. Subsequent unites retained the same reverse design and the obverses had a crowned bust of Charles I. Those of Cromwell and Charles II had the head encircled by a laurel wreath. It should be noted that the Cromwell reverse also showed his own particular version of the arms of the United Kingdom. (See ROYAL ARMS). Also, the unites of Charles I issued at the provincial mints of Oxford and Bristol bore the 'declaration' on the reverse instead of the shield (see DECLARATION TYPE). Two types of extremely rare octagonal unites were struck as siege pieces at Pontefract in the name of Charles II, for his father had already been beheaded.

The unite was always minted in 22 carat gold and except for the period from 1611 to 1619, when the currency was revalued by 10 per cent, it always circulated for 20s. (£1). As a successor to the pound sovereign, which James I struck in his first coinage, the unite underwent an immediate reduction in weight. The sovereign had 172 grains and the unite was 17 grains less. From 1619 it was $140\frac{1}{2}$ grains and in the reign of Charles II it was further reduced to $131\frac{3}{4}$ grains.

James I and Charles I also struck separate unites for circulation in Scotland, where they were worth £12. In design the unites of both monarchs differed little from the first British issues except that the king wore a Scottish crown and the shield on the reverse which, after being identical to the British version (the crown above it in this case was also a Scottish one) for the first few years, changed to the Scottish type with the Scottish lion in the first and fourth quarters and the English arms taking their place in the second.

Incidentally, the last Scottish unite of Charles I had the legend HIS PRAESVM VT PROSIM ("I am set over them, that I may be profitable to them").

Fractions of the unite were issued in both countries and usually went under different names: half-unite, double crown, quarter-unite, Britain crown, eighth of unite, Britain half-crown or half-crown.

See also TRIPLE UNITE, DOUBLE CROWN, BRITAIN CROWN.

V

VEILED HEAD   The unpopular jubilee coinage of Victoria was discontinued in 1893 and a more matronly portrait of the ageing Queen, wearing a partially veiled coronet, was designed for the silver and gold denominations by Thomas Brock, and his initials appeared below the bust. IND. IMP., signifying the

99. Veiled Head Sovereign of Victoria (obverse), and ×2

Queen's title of Empress of India, which she had received in 1877, appeared for the first time in the legend on her coins. This portrait superseded the 'young head' design on bronze coins in 1895.

VIGO   In 1702 during the War of Spanish Succession the British fleet, commanded by Admiral Sir George Rooke, carried off the treasure of gold and silver bullion which the Spanish

100. Shilling of 1702 (obverse) with VIGO inscription

ships had just brought back to Spain from South America and Mexico. The successful attack was carried out by British and Dutch ships at Vigo Bay, which is situated on the Spanish coast, north of Portugal, near to the Bay of Biscay. The bullion was brought back to England where it was to be turned into coins at the Royal Mint. To show the source of the metal, VIGO appeared below the bust of Queen Anne. In all other respects the coins struck were identical to the normal issues. Vigo shillings appeared in 1702, and the following year crowns, half-crowns and sixpences were also minted from the silver. In 1703 five guineas, guineas, and half-guineas were coined from the captured gold.

VOCE POPVLI The origin of this series of Irish tokens, which appeared in the 1760s, still remains a mystery, but it is considered by some that these issues of copper halfpennies, and some farthings, were struck by supporters of Charles Edward Stuart, the Young Pretender, who attempted unsuccessfully to capture the English throne with the help of his Scottish troops.

101. Voce Popvli Halfpenny (obverse)

Another opinion is that they were simply a token issue which was to circulate until the next regal coins arrived from England. It is safe to say, however, that the portrait, surrounded by the legend VOCE POPVLI ("By the voice of the people"), hardly resembled George III, the new king. The laureate bust was more like his grandfather, George II, except for the fact that it pointed in the wrong direction. The reverses showed a seated Hibernia with a spear, olive branch and harp, with her name above and the date in the exergue, not unlike the Irish coins of George I. Later, many of these coins circulated in the American colonies as an accepted form of currency.

W

W.C.C.   The Welsh Copper Company supplied the Royal Mint with silver bullion, which was coined into shillings from 1723 to

102. Shilling of 1723–26 (obverse) with WCC inscription

1726. The initials of the company appeared under the King's bust and plumes and interlinked CCs in alternate angles of the shields on the reverse.

WINDOW TAX   This tax, levied on houses which had six or more windows, was introduced in 1695 by William III's government, to offset the £2m. deficit the Mint had incurred by exchanging for face value, instead of weight, old hammered coins for new milled pieces, in an effort to demonetize the former currency. Naturally, many hammered coins were well-worn or clipped and bore no comparison to the new coins in weight. The tax was not repealed until 1851.

WIRE MONEY   The second issue of Maundy money struck by George III in 1792 had thin, wiry numerals on the reverse and was therefore termed 'wire money'.

WOLSEY'S GROAT   Six years after his quarrel with the Pope on the question of divorce, Henry VIII made himself Head of the Church in England with the Act of Supremacy in 1535, and at the same time abolished the privilege which the lords temporal, especially those at Canterbury, York and Durham, had held, of minting their own silver coins (gold was not permitted to be struck). The ecclesiastical mints were restricted to coining the smaller denominations of half-groat, penny and halfpenny. An exception was York, which issued groats while Cardinal Wolsey,

Chancellor and personal adviser to Henry VIII, was archbishop there from 1514 to 1530.

The obverse of the groat showed a profile of Henry, the reverse a long cross running between the quarters of the shield and bearing the royal arms in the centre. It was similar to the normal issue except that the initials TW for Thomas Wolsey appeared in the field on either side of the upper part of the shield, and a cardinal's hat below the royal arms. The same motifs were on the Wolsey half groats of York and the sovereign-type pennies of both York and Durham (from 1523 to 1529 Wolsey was also Bishop of Durham).

103. Wolsey Groat (reverse), and ×2

It was the groats to which the King took exception, for he considered Wolsey had usurped the royal prerogative by issuing them, and therefore, after his arrest for high treason, this was one of the charges brought against him. However, he died on the way to trial on 29th November 1530 and so was spared possible sentence of death.

WOOD'S IRISH COINAGE In 1722 William Wood of Bristol received the patent granted by George I to his mistress, the Duchess of Kendal, to mint over £100,000 worth of copper halfpennies and farthings for use in Ireland. Although they were the first coins for Ireland since 1696 and were of a high standard of workmanship, they were unpopular because of the huge profit being made by the manufacturer. Jonathan Swift, the Dean of St

Patrick's Cathedral in Dublin, was Wood's most outspoken opponent, and voiced his objections in the letters he wrote under the pseudonym of Drapier, calling for a boycott of the coins. So much embarrassment was caused to the British government that Wood was asked to surrender his patent in 1725, but he received a pension of £3,000 per annum from the Irish treasury as compensation. The coins were struck in fairly large quantities from 1722 to 1724, after which many were shipped to the North American colonies to be used as currency there. Later, Wood supplied other issues to these colonies in the *Rosa Americana* series.

The Irish coinage had two distinct types. The early coins of 1722 showed a laureate bust of the King facing right with GEORGIUS DEI GRATIA REX on the obverse, and a seated Hibernia holding a harp on her right and the legend HIBERNIA 1722 on the reverse. The second type, from 1722 to 1724, had a change in the reverse design. Hibernia's whole body faced more to the right, her left arm resting on her harp and her raised right hand holding a palm branch.

WYON The Wyon family is the most famous in the field of British medallic and numismatic art. For generations various members of the family became respected artists or sculptors. The Wyons were of German origin. Peter George Wyon (1710–44), a die-engraver, resided in Cologne and came to England in 1727 at the time of George II's accession to the throne.

Peter George's son, George (1735–97), became a modeller and die-engraver at Matthew Boulton's Soho factory in Birmingham. Each of his sons became notable die-engravers in that city too, but one son, Thomas (1767–1830), moved to London to be appointed Chief Engraver of His Majesty's Seals. His son, Thomas Jr (1792–1817), went to even greater heights, becoming Chief Engraver at the Royal Mint. He is most famous for the George III 'bull head' half-crown.

Thomas Jr's cousin, William (1795–1851), became Chief Engraver in 1828. His best known piece is a medal commemorating Queen Victoria's first official visit to the City of London in 1837. The Queen's portrait was used for the obverse of the 'young head' pieces and for Britain's first postage stamps in 1840. He designed many coins which circulated from the reign of George IV to that of Victoria.

When William Wyon died, one of his two sons, Leonard Charles (1826–91), the last of the famous Wyons, became the next Chief Engraver at the Mint. Among his many designs, L. C. Wyon is most famous for his design of the 'bun-head' portrait on copper coins from 1860–95.

See also INITIALS.

Y

YOUNG HEAD This term was given to the first portrait of Queen Victoria which appeared, with only slight modifications, on her gold and silver coinage until 1887, when the 'jubilee head' was introduced; and on copper and bronze coins until 1895, when it was superseded by the more suitable 'veiled head'. By this time the Queen was seventy years old. The 'young head' did not appear on the second issue of the crown in 1847 or on any florin from 1849 to 1887, a Gothic-style portrait being preferred.

104. Young Head Sovereign of Victoria (obverse)

The 'young head' portrait, designed by the Royal Mint's Chief Engraver, William Wyon, showed the Queen's uncrowned head with her hair gathered high at the back and bound with two ribbons.

APPENDIX I

Glossary of Numismatic Terms

assay	to test the exactness of weight and purity of a metal.
brockage	a mis-strike when a coin has the same design on both sides – one normal, the other inverted; this is caused by one coin remaining in the press and acting as a die for one side of the next one.
blank	a metal shape of a coin that has not been struck yet.
clipping	the removing of metal from the edge of a coin, normally one of precious metal.
coinage design	obverse and reverse not the same way up; after one side has been struck, the flan is turned through usually 180 degrees before the other is stamped.
countermark	extra stamp on a coin usually made at a later date to change or guarantee its value.
cruciform	elements of design in the shape of a cross of St George (+).
cuirassed	in armour.
device	the design on a coin.
die	stamp or punch used to strike a coin.
draped	the shoulder and chest covered by a toga type of garment.
engrailed	descriptive term for the edge of a coin which has a series of dots or curved lines on it.
exergue	segment below the main design and usually cut off from it to display the date or value of a piece.
field	part of the obverse or reverse of a coin which contains no design.
flan	same as 'blank'.
frosting	parts of the design on proofs and patterns that have been dulled.
graining	the serrations on the edge of a coin (see also main part of handbook).
hammered coinage	coins struck by hand (see main part of book).
incuse	legend or design which is impressed into the blank (opposite of 'relief').
jugate	two or more busts side by side and overlapping.

laureate	with laurel leaves.
legend	wording on a coin.
medal design	obverse and reverse the same way up.
milled coinage	coins struck by machine (see main part of book).
milling	see 'graining'.
money of account	units of money used in accounting; no coins of these amounts are struck.
mule	a coin which does not have a matching obverse and reverse.
obverse	portrait side of a coin, in the absence of a portrait the titles, legends or motifs common to the series. Often called 'heads'.
overstrike	new design struck over an old one.
pattern	(see main part of book).
pile	lower die in hammered coinage.
planchet	same as 'blank'.
proof	(see main part of book).
quatrefoil	same as 'cruciform'.
relief	raised legend or design (opposite of 'incuse').
reverse	the opposite side to the obverse of a coin, often called 'tails'.
rim	raised line around the circumference of the coin to protect the design from wear.
saltire	elements of design in the shape of a cross of St Andrew (X).
truncation	place where the bust is cut off.
trussel	upper die in hammered coinage.
uniface	design only on one side of a blank.
vis à vis	portraits placed face to face on a coin.
Z	an abbreviation for 'and' found in legends.

Monarchs of England and Great Britain

There were various kingdoms in England (*e.g.*, Mercia, Northumbria). Egbert, the sixteenth King of Wessex is considered the first King of all England.

Egbert	802–839
Ethelwulf	839–858
Ethelbald	858–860
Ethelbert	860–865
Ethelred I	865–871
Alfred the Great	871–899
Edward the Elder	899–924
Athelstan	924–939
Edmund I	939–946
Edred	946–955
Edwy	955–959
Edgar	959–975
Edward the Younger	975–978
Ethelred II (the Unready)	978–1016
Edmund II	1016
Canute	1016–1035
Harthacanute & Harold I	1035
Harold I	1035–1040
Harthacanute	1040–1042
Edward the Confessor	1042–1066
Harold II	1066

House of Normandy

William I	1066–1087
William II	1087–1100
Henry I	1100–1135
Stephen	1135–1154

House of Plantagenet

Henry II	1154–1189
Richard I	1189–1199
John	1199–1216
Henry III	1216–1272
Edward I	1272–1307
Edward II	1307–1327
Edward III	1327–1377
Richard II	1377–1399

House of Lancaster
    Henry IV   1399–1413
    Henry V   1413–1422
    Henry VI   1422–1461

House of York
    Edward IV   1461–1470
    (Henry VI again   1470–1471)
    Edward IV   1471–1483
    Edward V   1483
    Richard III   1483–1485

House of Tudor
    Henry VII   1485–1509
    Henry VIII   1509–1547
    Edward VI   1547–1553
    Mary   1553–1554
    Mary & Philip   1554–1558
    Elizabeth I   1558–1603

House of Stuart
    James I   1603–1625
    Charles I   1625–1649
    (Commonwealth   1649–1660
    Charles II   1660–1685
    James II   1685–1688

House of Orange
    William & Mary   1688–1694
    William III   1694–1702

House of Stuart
    Anne   1702–1714

House of Hanover
    George I   1714–1727
    George II   1727–1760
    George III   1760–1820
    George IV   1820–1830
    William IV   1830–1837
    Victoria   1837–1901

House of Saxe-Coburg-Gotha
    Edward VII   1901–1911

House of Windsor

George V	1911–1936
Edward VIII	1936
George VI	1936–1952
Elizabeth II	1952–

Monarchs of Scotland

Constantine I	789–820
Kenneth I	832–860
Donald	860–863
Constantine II	863–877
Eocha	881–889
Donald I	889–900
Constantine III	900–942
Malcolm I	942–954
Indulf	954–962
Dubh	962–967
Cuilean	967–971
Kenneth II	971–995
Constantine IV	995–997
Kenneth III	997–1005
Malcolm II	1005–1034
Duncan	1034–1040
Macbeth	1040–1057
Lulach	1057–1058
Malcolm III	1058–1093
Donald Bane	1093
Duncan II	1094
Donald Bane – again ⎫ Edmund ⎭	1094–1097
Edgar	1097–1107
Alexander I	1107–1124
David I	1124–1153
Malcolm IV	1153–1165
William I (the Lion)	1165–1214
Alexander II	1214–1249
Alexander III	1249–1286
Margaret	1286–1290
(Interregnum	1290–1292
John Baliol	1292–1296
(Interregnum	1296–1306
Robert I (the Bruce)	1306–1329
David II	1329–1371
Robert II	1371–1390
Robert III	1390–1406
James I	1406–1437
James II	1437–1460

James III	1460–1488
James IV	1488–1513
James V	1513–1542
Mary	1542–1567
James VI	1567–1603

James VI became James I of England in 1603. From that date the sovereigns of both countries were the same. However, James II of England was James VII of Scotland and William III was William II 'north of the border'.

Museums with Coin and Medal Collections

The only comprehensive guide to museums in Great Britain and Northern Ireland is *Museums and Art Galleries*. This annual publication gives an index of places where collections of coins and medals are on display. The following list of museums with addresses and telephone numbers is reproduced here with the kind permission of ABC Historic Publications, the publishers of *Museums and Art Galleries in Great Britain and Northern Ireland*.

Whilst every care has been taken in compiling this list, it does not claim to be complete. Admission fees and opening times have been omitted as these are very often subject to alteration. For security reasons some collections are not on general display but can be viewed by members of the public after making arrangements with the curators of the museums.

ABERDEEN	Aberdeen University Anthropological Museum, Tel: 0224–40241 Ext. 243M.
	Aberdeen Art Gallery, 61 Schoolhill, Aberdeen. Tel: 0224–26333.
ABERYSTWYTH	Ceredigion Museum, Coliseum, Terrace Road, Aberystwyth, Dyfed. Tel: 0970–617911.
ABINGDON	Abingdon Museum, The County Hall, Market Place, Abingdon, Oxon. Tel: 0235–23703.
ACCRINGTON	Haworth Art Gallery, Haworth Park, Accrington, Lancs. Tel: 0254–33782.
ALDBOROUGH	The Aldborough Roman Museum, Aldborough, Boroughbridge, N. Yorks. Tel: 090–122768.
ASHWELL	Ashwell Village Museum, Swan Street, Ashwell, Herts.
AXBRIDGE	Axbridge Museum, King John's Hunting Lodge, The Square, Axbridge, Somerset. Tel: 0934–732012.
AYLESBURY	Buckinghamshire County Museum, Church Street, Aylesbury, Bucks. Tel: 0296–82158 and 88849.
BASINGSTOKE	The Willis Museum & Art Gallery, New Street, Basingstoke, Hants. Tel: 0256–65902.

BATH	Holburne of Menstrie Museum, Great Pulteney Street, Bath, Avon. Tel: 0225–66669.
	Victoria Art Gallery, Bridge Street, Bath, Avon. Tel: 0225–61111 Ext. 418.
	Roman Baths Museum, Abbey Churchyard, Near Bath Abbey, Bath, Avon. Tel: 0225–61111 Ext. 327.
	American Museum In Britain, Claverton Manor, Nr. Bath, Avon. Tel: 0225–60503.
BEDFORD	Bedford Museum, Castle Lane, Bedford. Tel: 0234–53323.
BIRMINGHAM	Birmingham City Museum & Art Gallery, Chamberlain Square, Birmingham 3. Tel: 021–235–2834. (Dept. of Local History & Dept. of Archaeology and Ethnography.)
BLACKBURN	Blackburn Museum & Art Gallery, Library Street, Blackburn, Lancs. Tel: 0254–667130.
BOLTON	Museum & Art Gallery, Civic Centre, Bolton, Greater Manchester. Tel: 0204–22311 Ext. 379.
BOURNEMOUTH	Russell-Cotes Art Gallery & Museum, East Cliff, Bournemouth, Dorset. Tel: 0202–21009.
BRIGHTON	Brighton Museum & Art Gallery, Church Street, Brighton, East Sussex. Tel: 0273–603005.
	The Thomas-Stanford Museum, Preston Manor, Preston Park, Brighton, East Sussex. Tel: 0273–552101.
	The Royal Pavilion, Brighton, East Sussex. Tel: 0273–603005.
BRISTOL	City of Bristol Museum & Art Gallery, Queen's Road, Bristol 8, Avon. Tel: 0272–299771.
CALDERDALE	Bankfield Museum & Art Gallery, Halifax, West Yorks. Tel: 0422–54823.
CAMBRIDGE	Fitzwilliam Museum, Trumpington Street, Cambridge. Tel: 0223–69501–3.
CANTERBURY	The Royal Museum & Art Gallery, The Beaney, High Street, Canterbury, Kent. Tel: 0227–52747.
CARDIFF	The National Museum of Wales, Cardiff, South Glamorgan. Tel: 0222–397951.

CARMARTHEN	The Carmarthen Museum, Abergwili, Dyfed. Tel: 0267–31691.
CHELMSFORD	Chelmsford & Essex Museum, Oaklands Park, Moulsham Street, Chelmsford, Essex. Tel: 0245–60614.
CHESTER	Grosvenor Museum, Grosvenor Street, Chester, Cheshire. Tel: 0244–21616.
COLNE	British in India Museum, Sun Street, Colne, Lancs.
COVENTRY	Herbert Art Gallery & Museum, Jordan Well, Coventry, West Midlands. Tel: 0203–25555, Ext. 2662.
	Lunt Roman Fort, Baginton, Coventry, West Midlands. Tel: 0203–25555, Ext. 2662.
DOVER	Dover Museum, Ladywell, Dover, Kent. Tel: 0304–201066.
DUMFRIES	Dumfries Museum, The Observatory, Corberry Hill, Dumfries. Tel: 0387–3374.
EDINBURGH	National Museum of Antiquities of Scotland, Queen Street, Edinburgh 2. Tel: 031–556–8921.
	Royal Scottish Museum, Chambers Street, Edinburgh 1. Tel: 031–225–7534.
EXETER	Royal Albert Memorial Museum & Art Gallery, Queen Street, Exeter, Devon. Tel: 0392–56724.
GLASGOW	The Hunterian Museum, Glasgow University, Glasgow 12. Tel: 041–339–8855 Ext. 221.
	Art Gallery & Museum, Kelvingrove, Glasgow. Tel: 041–334–1134/5/6.
GLENESK	Glenesk Museum, The Retreat, Glenesk, Angus. Tel: 03567–236.
GLOUCESTER	City Museum & Art Gallery, Brunswick Road, Gloucester. Tel: 0452–24131.
HASTINGS	Museum & Art Gallery, Cambridge Road, Hastings, East Sussex. Tel: 0424–435952.
HAVERFORDWEST	The Castle Museum & Art Gallery, Haverfordwest, Dyfed. Tel: 0437–3708.
HAWICK	Museum & Art Gallery, Wilton Lodge Park, Hawick, Roxburgh. Tel: 0450–3457.
HITCHIN	Hitchin Museum & Art Gallery, Paynes Park, Hitchin, Herts. Tel: 0462–4476.

HOLYWELL	The Grange Cavern Military Museum, Grange Lane, Holway, Nr. Holywell, Clwyd. Tel: 0352–713455.
HOVE	Hove Museum of Art, 19 New Church Road, Hove, East Sussex. Tel: 0273–779410.
HULL	Wilberforce House & Georgian Houses, 23–25 High Street, Hull, Humberside. Tel: 0482–223111 Ext. 2737.
IPSWICH	Ipswich Museum, High Street, Ipswich, Suffolk. Tel: 0473–213761–2.
JERSEY	Elizabeth Castle, St Helier, Jersey. Tel: 0534–23971.
	Mont Orgueil Castle, Gorey, Jersey. Tel: 0534–53292.
KENDAL	Kendal Museum of Archaeology & Natural History, Station Road, Kendal, Cumbria. Tel: 0539–21374.
KIDDERMINSTER	Museum, Kidderminster, Hereford & Worcester. Tel: 0562–66610.
KILMARNOCK	Dick Institute Museum & Art Gallery, Elmbank Avenue, Kilmarnock, Ayrshire. Tel: 0563–26401.
KING'S LYNN	The Lynn Museum, King's Lynn, Norfolk. Tel: 0553–5001.
LEICESTER	The Newarke Houses Museum, The Newarke, Leicester. Tel: 0533–554100.
LETCHWORTH	Museum & Art Gallery, Broadway, Letchworth, Herts. Tel: 04626–5647.
LEWES	Barbican House Museum, High Street, Lewes, East Sussex. Tel: 07916–4379.
LICHFIELD	Lichfield Art Gallery, Bird Street, Lichfield, Staffs. Tel: 05432–2177.
LINCOLN	Usher Gallery, Lindum Road, Lincoln. Tel: 0522–27980.
LONDON	British Museum, Great Russell Street, London WC1. Tel: 01–636–1555.
	Forty Hall, Forty Hill, Enfield. Tel: 01–363–8196.
	Gunnersbury Park Museum, Gunnersbury Park, London W3. Tel: 01–992–1612.
	Jewish Museum, Woburn House, Upper Woburn Place, London WC1. Tel: 01–387–3081.
	Kingston-upon-Thames Museum & Art

Gallery, Fairfield West, Kingston-upon-Thames, Surrey. Tel: 01–546–5386.

Imperial War Museum, Lambeth Road, London SE1. Tel: 01–735–8922.

National Maritime Museum, Romney Road, Greenwich, London SE10. Tel: 01–858–4422.

Royal Air Force Museum, Aerodrome Road, Hendon, London NW9. Tel: 01–205–2266.

Royal Hospital Museum, Royal Hospital, Royal Hospital Road, Chelsea, London SW3. Tel: 01–730–0161.

St John's Gate, St John's Square, Clerkenwell, London EC1. Tel: 01–253–6644.

LUTON	Luton Museum & Art Gallery, Wardown Park, Luton, Beds. Tel: 0582–36941–2.
MACCLESFIELD	West Park Museum & Art Gallery, Prestbury Road, Macclesfield, Cheshire. Tel: 0625–24067 or 0606–41331.
MAIDSTONE	Museum & Art Gallery, St Faith's Street, Maidstone, Kent. Tel: 0622–54497.
MALMESBURY	Athelstan Museum, Cross Hayes, Malmesbury, Wilts. Tel: 06662–2143.
MANCHESTER	Manchester Museum, The University, Oxford Road, Manchester. Tel: 061–273–3333.
MANSFIELD	Mansfield Museum & Art Gallery, Leeming Street, Mansfield, Notts. Tel: 0623–22561 Ext. 264.
MERTHYR TYDFIL	Art Gallery & Museum, Cyfarthfa Castle, Merthyr Tydfil, Mid Glamorgan. Tel: 0685–3112.
MIDDLESBROUGH	Dorman Museum, Linthorpe Road, Middlesbrough, Cleveland. Tel: 0642–813781.
MONTROSE	Montrose Museum, Panmure Place, Montrose, Angus. Tel: 0674–3232.
NORTHAMPTON	Abington Museum, Abington Park, Northampton. Tel: 0604–32454.
NORTHWICH	Salt Museum, London Road, Northwich, Cheshire.
NORWICH	Norwich Castle Museum, Norwich, Norfolk. Tel: 0603–611277 Ext. 279.
NOTTINGHAM	Nottingham Castle Museum, Nottingham.

Tel: 0602–411881.

NUNEATON Nuneaton Museum & Art Gallery, Riversley Park, Nuneaton, Warwickshire. Tel: 0682–382683.

OXFORD The Ashmolean Museum of Art & Archaeology, Beaumont Street, Oxford. Tel: 0865–512651.

PETERHEAD Arbuthnot Museum, St Peter Street, Peterhead, Aberdeenshire. Tel: 0779–77778.

PORTSMOUTH Point Museum, The Round Tower, Broad Street, Portsmouth, Hants.

READING Museum & Art Gallery, Blagrave Street, Reading, Berkshire. Tel: 0734–55911 Ext. 2242.

ST IVES Norris Museum, The Broadway, St Ives, Cambridgeshire. Tel: 0480–65101.

SALFORD Ordsall Hall Museum, Taylorson Street, Salford, Greater Manchester. Tel: 061–872–0251.

SALISBURY Salisbury & South Wiltshire Museum, The King's House, 65 The Close, Salisbury, Wilts. Tel: 0722–332151.

SHEFFIELD Sheffield City Museum, Weston Park, Sheffield 10. Tel: 0742–27226–7.

SHUGBOROUGH Staffordshire County Museum & Mansion House, Shugborough, Nr Stafford. Tel: 0889–881388.

SPALDING Spalding Museum, Broad Street, Spalding, Lincs. Tel: 0775–4658.

STOCKTON-ON-TEES Preston Hall Museum, Preston Park, Eaglescliffe, Stockton-on-Tees, Cleveland. Tel: 0642–781184.

STROUD Stroud Museum, Lansdown, Stroud, Glos. Tel: 04536–3394.

SWANSEA University College of Swansea & Royal Institution of South Wales Museum (Swansea Museum), Victoria Road, Swansea, West Glamorgan. Tel: 0792–53763.

SWINDON Museum & Art Gallery, Bath Road, Swindon, Wilts. Tel: 0793–26161 Ext. 3129.

TAMWORTH Tamworth Castle Museum, The Holloway, Tamworth, Staffs. Tel: 0827–4222.

THETFORD The Ancient House Museum, White Hart

	Street, Thetford, Norfolk. Tel: 0842–2599.
TIVERTON	The Tiverton Museum, St Andrew Street, Tiverton, Devon. Tel: 0884–256295 or 0884–255446.
WARRINGTON	Museum & Art Gallery, Bold Street, Warrington, Cheshire. Tel: 0925–30550.
WARWICK	Warwickshire Museum, Market Place, Warwick. Tel: 0926–43431 Ext. 2500; (Sat.) 42778.
WELLS	Wells Museum, Cathedral Green, Wells, Somerset. Tel: 0749–73477.
WINCHCOMBE	Hailes Abbey Museum, Hailes Abbey, Winchcombe, Glos. Tel: 0242–602398.
YEOVIL	Wyndham Museum, Hendford Manor Hall, Yeovil, Somerset. Tel: 0935–5171; (Sat.) 24774.

Periodicals

The following is a list of numismatic periodicals published in the British Isles.

1. *Coin and Medal Bulletin* – monthly magazine from B. A. Seaby Ltd, available on subscription only. Contains articles on numismatics and a catalogue of coins offered for sale by B. A. Seaby Ltd, Audley House, 11 Margaret Street, London W1N 8AT.
2. *Coin and Medal News* – monthly magazine on coins, medals, banknotes and tokens published by Epic Publishing Ltd. (UK), PO Box 3DE, London W1A 3DE.
3. *Coins: Market Values* – annual publication concentrating on coin prices and including a few articles mainly on investment. Link House Magazines (Croydon) Ltd, Dingwall Avenue, Croydon, Surrey.
4. *Coin Monthly* – monthly magazine on coins, medals, banknotes and tokens published by Numismatic Publishing Co., Sovereign House, Brentwood, Essex, CM14 4SE.
5. *Coin Year Book* – annual publication of *Coin Monthly* with articles on coins, medals and banknotes, directories of dealers, societies *etc.*, and price lists of British coins. Numismatic Publishing Co.
6. *Irish Numismatics* – magazine published by Stagecast Publications of Dublin. Six issues per year devoted to Irish numismatics. Stagecast Publications, 15 Eaton Square, Monkstown, Dublin, Eire.
7. *The Numismatic Circular* – monthly magazine published by Spink & Son Ltd, available on subscription only. Contains articles on numismatics and coins offered for sale by Spink & Son Ltd, King Street, St James's, London SW1.

Bibliography

The following is a list of books on the coins, coinages and tokens of the British Isles. As is evident from the titles, some are of a specialist nature dealing only with a particular aspect or period of British numismatics. Certain books are not concerned solely with British coins, yet they have been included in this bibliography because of the amount of space they devote to the subject. Although the bibliography is comprehensive, containing a number of books which are out of print and only available in the larger or specialist libraries, it makes no claim to be complete. All of the books have been published in the British Isles unless otherwise stated.

In addition, it must not be forgotten that some of the best and most up to date information on British numismatics can be found in the *British Numismatic Journal* and the *Numismatic Chronicle*, the annual publications of the British Numismatic Society and the Royal Numismatic Society respectively.

Coins

Allen, D. F., *Catalogue of English Coins in the British Museum: Cross and Crosslet ("Tealby") Type of Henry II* (1951). British Museum

Amstell, M., *The Early Period in Coin Collecting Edward II to 130 B.C.* (1970)

——, *Another Period in Coin Collecting: Charles I – Edward III* (1967)

——, *A Start to Coin Collecting: Elizabeth II to Charles II* (1966). Foulsham

Askew, G., *The Coinage of Roman Britain* (1951, 2nd edition 1980). Seaby

Becker, T., *The Coin Makers* (U.S.A. 1969). Oak Tree Press

Beresford-Jones R. D., *A Manual of Anglo-Gallic Gold Coins* (1964). Spink

Boundy, W. S., *Bushell and Harman of Lundy* (1961)

Bramah, E., *English Regal Copper Coins: Charles II to Victoria: 1671–1860* (1929). Methuen

Bressett, K. E., *Guide Book of English Coins: Nineteenth & Twentieth Centuries* (U.S.A., 4th ed. 1965). Whitman

Brooke, G. C., *English Coinage from the Seventh Century to the Present Day* (3rd edition 1951)

——, *Catalogue of English Coins in the British Museum: Norman Kings* – 2 vols. (1916). Methuen

Brown, I. D. and Dolley R. H. M., *A Bibliography of Coin Hoards of Great Britain & Ireland: 1500–1967* (1971). Spink

Burns, E., *The Coinage of Scotland* – 2 vols. (1887). A & C Black

Carson, R. A. G., *Coins* – 3 vols: Vol. 2 "Coins of Europe" (1971)
—— (Editor), *Mints, Dies & Currency* (1971). Hutchinson

Challis, C. E., *The Tudor Coinage* (1978). Manchester University Press

Chamberlain, C. C., *The World of Coins: A Dictionary of Numismatics* (1976). English University Press

Cochran-Patrick, R. W., *Records of the Coinage of Scotland from the Earliest Period to the Union* – 2 vols. (1876)

Coffey, G., *A Guide to the Collection of Irish Antiquities: Anglo-Irish Coins* (1911)

Cope, G. M. and Raynor, P. A., *The Standard Catalogue of English Milled Coinage in Silver, Copper & Bronze, 1662–1972* (1975). Spink

Craig, Sir J., *The Mint: A History of the London Mint from A.D. 287 to 1948* (1953). Cambridge University Press

Crowther, R. F., *A Guide to English Pattern Coins in Gold, Silver, Copper & Pewter from Edward I to Victoria* (1887)

Dickinson, H. W., *Matthew Boulton* (1937). Cambridge University Press

Dolley, R. H. M., *Anglo-Saxon Pennies* (1964, reprinted 1970). British Museum

——, *Anglo-Saxon Coins: Studies Presented to F. M. Stenton on the Occasion of his 80th Birthday (17.5.60)* (1961) Methuen

——, *Mediaeval Anglo-Irish Coins* (1972). Seaby

——, *The Norman Conquest and the English Coinage* (1966). Spink

——, *Viking Coins of the Danelaw and of Dublin* (1965). British Museum

Dowle, A. and Finn, P., *The Guide Book to the Coinage of Ireland from A.D. 995 to the Present Day* (1969). Spink

Duveen, Sir G. and Stride, H. G., *History of the Gold Sovereign* (1962). Oxford University Press

Dyer, G. P., *The Proposed Coinage of King Edward VIII* (1973 – a publication of H.M.S.O.)

Edmundson, J., *Collecting Modern British Coins* (1970). Pelham

Evans, J., *Coins of the Ancient Britons* (1864 and supplement of 1890). J. R. Smith

Exley, W., *Guernsey Coinage* (1969)

Feavearyear, Sir. A., *The Pound Sterling. A History of English Money* (London 2nd revised edition 1963). Oxford University Press

Frey, A. R., *Dictionary of Numismatic Names with Addenda* (U.S.A. 1917, reprint 1973). Spink

Folkes, M., *Tables of English Silver and Gold Coins* (1768)

Freeman, M. J., *The Victorian Bronze Penny (1860–1901)* (1970)

Friedberg, R., *Coins of the British World (Complete from A.D. 500 to the Present)* (U.S.A. 1962). Ryerson

Gould, J. D., *The Great Debasement: Currency and the Economy in Mid-Tudor England* (1970). Cambridge University Press

Grueber, H. A., *Handbook of the Coins of Great Britain and Ireland in the British Museum* (1899, revised edition 1970). Spink Museum

Hawkins, E., *Silver Coins of England* (3rd edition 1887, reprinted 1975). Firecress Publishing Company

Henfrey, H. W., *A Guide to the Study and Arrangement of English Coins Giving a Description of Every Denomination of Every Issue in Gold, Silver and Copper from the Conquest to the Present Time with all the Latest Discoveries* (1870 – also revised edition 1885). J. R. Smith

——, *Numismata Cromwelliana or the Medallic History of Oliver Cromwell – Coins, Medals and Seals* (1877). J. R. Smith

Henry, J., *The Series of English Coins in Copper, Tin and Bronze* (1879)

Hewlett, L. M., *Anglo-Gallic Coins* (1920). A. H. Baldwin & Sons

Johnson, R. F., *Coin Collecting. A Beginner's Guide* (1968). Lutterworth Press

Josset, C. R., *Money in Britain. A History of the Currencies of the British Isles* (1962). Warne

Keary, C. F. and Grueber, H. A., *A Catalogue of English Coins in the British Museum. Vol. 2: Wessex and England to the Norman Conquest* (1893). British Museum

Keary, C. F. and Poole R. S., *A Catalogue of English Coins in the British Museum. Vol 1: Anglo-Saxon Series* (1887) British Museum

Kelly, E. M., *Spanish Dollars and Silver Tokens, an Account of the Issues of the Bank of England 1797–1816* (1976). Spink

Kent, J., *2,000 Years of British Coins & Medals* (1978). British Museum.

Kenyon, R. L., *Gold Coins of England* (1884, reprinted 1970). Quaritch

Li, Ming-Hsun, *The Great Recoinage of 1696–1699* (1963). Weidenfeld & Nicolson

Lindsay, J., *A View of the Coinage of the Heptarchy to which is Added a List of Unpublished Mints and Moneyers of Chief or Sole Monarchs from Egbert to Harold II* (1842). Hearne
——, *A View of the Coinage of Ireland from the Invasion of the Danes to the Reign of George IV* (1839). Hearne
——, *A View of the Coinage of Scotland with Copious Lists, Descriptions and Extracts from Acts of Parliament* (1845, with supplement, 1859). Hearne

Linecar, H. W. A., *Advanced Guide to Coin Collecting* (1970). Pelham
——, *Beginners Guide to Coin Collecting* (1966). Pelham
——, *British Coin Designs and Designers* (1977). Bell
——, *Coins* (1962). Benn
——, *Coin and Medal Collecting for Pleasure and Profit* (1971). Pelham
——, *Coins and Medals* (1971). Hamlyn
——, *The Crown Pieces of Great Britain and the British Commonwealth of Nations 1551–1961* (1969). Spink
——, *The Observer's Book of Coins* (1977). Warne
——, Editor of *Milled Coinage of England 1662–1946* (1966). Spink

Linecar, H. W. A. and Stone, A. G., *English Proof and Pattern Crown-Size Pieces 1658–1960* (1968). Spink

MacDonald, G., *Evolution of Coinage* (1916). Cambridge University Press

Mack, R. P., *The Coinage of Ancient Britain. Celtic Coinage* (1964, 3rd edition 1975). Spink

Mackay, J. A., *Encyclopaedia of Isle of Man Coins & Tokens* (1979)
——, *Value in Coins and Medals* (1970). Johnson

Mackenzie, A. D., *The Bank of England Note. A History of Its Printing* (1953). Cambridge University Press

Marsh, M.A., *The Gold Half-Sovereign* (1982)
——, *The Gold Sovereign* (1980)

Marshall, G., *A View of the Silver Coin and Coinage of Great Britain from the Year 1662–1837 Containing an Account of Every Denomination of Coin and Specifying Every Kind of Type, Legend and Date of Each Variety. Also an Account of the Silver Coins Struck in Scotland from the Year 1662 to the Union of the Two Kingdoms in 1707* (1838). Hearne

Montagu, H., *The Copper, Tin and Bronze Coinage and Patterns for Coins from the Reign of Elizabeth to that of her Present Majesty* (1893). Quaritch

Moore, N. E. A., *The Decimalisation of Britain's Currency* (1973 – a publication of H.M.S.O.)

Nathanson, A. J., *Thomas Simon. His Life and Work 1618–1665* (1975). Seaby

Nelson, P., *The Coinage of Ireland in Copper, Tin and Pewter 1460–1826* (1905)
——, *The Coinage of William Wood 1722–1733* (reprinted 1959 and 1978)
——, *The Obsidional Money of the Great Rebellion 1642–1649* (1907)

Newman, W. A. C., *British Coinage. Its History and Technology* (Monograph to the Royal Institute of Chemistry 1953)

North, J. J., *The Coinages of Edward I and II* (1968). Spink
——, *English Hammered Coinage Vol. 1 (c. 650–A.D. 1272)* (1964, 2nd edition 1980). Spink
——, *English Hammered Coinage Vol. 2 (A.D. 1272–1622)* (1960, 2nd edition 1976). Spink

Nolan, P., *A Monetary History of Ireland. Vol. 1: Ancient Ireland* (1926). P. S. King
——, *A Monetary History of Ireland. Vol. 2: Anglo-Norman Invasion to the Death of Elizabeth* (1928). P. S. King

Oman, C., *The Coinage of England* (1931, reprinted 1967). Oxford University Press

O'Sullivan, W., *The Earliest Irish Coinage* (1961)

Peck, C. W., *English Copper, Tin and Bronze Coins in the British Museum 1558–1963* (1964). British Museum

Petersson, H. B. A., *Anglo-Saxon Currency, King Edgar's Reform to the Norman Conquest* (1969)

Phillips, M., *Token Money of the Bank of England (1797–1816)* (1900). E. Wilson

Porteous, J., *Coins* (1973). Octopus Books
——, *Coins in History* (1969). Weidenfeld & Nicolson

Pridmore, F., *Coins of the British Commonwealth of Nations to the End of the Reign of George VI 1953. Part 1, European Territories* (1960). Spink

Purvey, P. F., *Coins and Tokens of Scotland* (1972). Seaby

Remick, J. H., *The Coinage of the Republic of Ireland 1926–1968* (1968)

Remick, J. H; Somer, J; Dowle, A and Finn, P., *The Guidebook and Catalogue of British Commonwealth Coins (1649–1971)* (1971). Regency Coin and Stamp Company

Richardson, A. B., *Scottish Coins* (1901, reprinted 1977)

Robertson, J. D., *A Handbook to the Coinage of Scotland Giving a Description of Every Variety Issued by the Scottish Mint in Gold, Silver, Billon and Copper from Alexander 1 to Anne* (1878)

Robinson, Dr B., *The Royal Maundy* (1977). Kaye & Ward

Royal Mint Report, *Annual Report of the Deputy Master and Comptroller* (published each financial year). H.M.S.O.

Ruding, R., *Annals of the Coinage of Great Britain and its Dependencies from the Earliest Period of Authentic History to the Reign of Victoria* (3 Vols, 3rd edition, 1840). H. Bohn

Seaby, H. A. (editor), *Notes on English Silver Coins 1066–1648* (1948). Seaby

Seaby, H. A. and Raynor, P. A., *The English Silver Coinage from 1649* (1968). Seaby

Seaby, P. J., *Coins and Tokens of Ireland* (1970). Seaby

——, *Standard Catalogue of British Coins* (Annual publication). Seaby

——, *The Story of the English Coinage* (1952). Seaby

Seaby, P. J. and Bussell, M., *British Copper Coins and their Values* (1969). Seaby

Smith, R. B., *The Anglo-Hanoverian Coinage* (1970)

Snelling, T., *On the Coins of Great Britain, France and Ireland* (1823)

Spink & Son Ltd, *The Milled Coinage of England 1662–1946* (1950). Spink

Stewart, I. H., *The Scottish Coinage* (1967, 2nd edition 1976). Spink

Sutherland, C. H. V., *Anglo-Saxon Gold Coinage in the Light of the Crondall Hoard* (1948)

——, *Art in Coinage. The Aesthetics of Money from Greece to the Present Day* (1955). Batsford

——, *Coinage and Currency in Roman Britain* (1937). Oxford University Press

——, *English Coinage (600–1900)* (1973). Batsford

——, *Gold* (revised edition 1969). Thames & Hudson

Sweeny, J. O., *A Numismatic History of the Birmingham Mint* (1981)

Sylloge of Coins of the British Isles (published in numerous parts since (1958). O.U.P. and Spink

Thompson, J. D. A., *Inventory of British Coin Hoards* A.D. *600–1500* (1956)

Thorburn, W. S., *Guide to the History and Valuation of the Coins of Great Britain and Ireland from the Earliest Period to the Present Time* (1898, revised and enlarged by H. E. Grueber in 1905). L. U. Gill

Trowbridge, R. J., *History, Coinage, Paper Notes and Medals of Edward VIII of Great Britain* (1970)

Went, A. E. J., *Irish Coins & Medals* (1978). Eason

Wingate, J., *Illustrations of the Coinage of Scotland* (1869)

Wright, P. A., *The Pictorial History of the Royal Maundy* (1968). Pitkin Pictorials Ltd

Young, D., *Coin Catalogue of Ireland 1722–1969* (1969). Stagecast Publications

Tokens

Atkins, J., *The Tradesmen's Tokens of the Eighteenth Century* (1892)

Batty, D. T., *Descriptive Catalogue of the Copper Coinage of Great Britain, Ireland, British Isles and Colonies, Local and Private Tokens, Jettons* etc. (4 vols. 1898)

Bell, R. C., *Commercial Coins 1787–1804* (1963). Corbitt & Hunter

——, *Copper Commercial Coins 1811–1819* (1964). Corbitt & Hunter

——, *Special Tokens and Those Struck for General Circulation 1784–1804* (1968). Corbitt & Hunter

——, *Tradesmen's Tickets and Private Tokens 1785–1819* (1966). Corbitt & Hunter

Berry, G., *Discovering Trade Tokens* (1969). Shire Publications

Dalton, R., *The Silver Token Coinage mainly Issued between 1811 and 1812* (1922, reprinted 1968). Seaby

Dalton, R. and Hamer, S. H., *The Provincial Token Coinage of the Eighteenth Century* (1910–1918, reprinted 1967 and 1977). Seaby

Davis, W. J., *The Nineteenth Century Token Coinage of Great Britain, Ireland, the Channel Islands and the Isle of Man to Which are Added Tokens of over One Penny Value of Any Period* (1904, reprinted 1969 and 1979). Seaby

Fuld, G. and M., *Token Collector's Pages* (1972)

Herdman, E. F., *Transport Tokens, Tickets, Passes and Badges of Great Britain and Ireland* (1932). Private publication

Kent, G C., *British Metallic Coins and Tradesmen's Tokens with their Value from 1600–1912* (1912). Private publication

Mathias, P., *English Trade Tokens. The Industrial Revolution Illustrated* (1962). Abelard-Schuman

Scott, J. G., *British Countermarks on Copper and Bronze Coins* (1975). Spink

Seaby, P. J. and Bussell, M., *British Tokens and their Values* (1970). Seaby

Waters, A. W., *Notes on Eighteenth Century Tokens* (1954). Seaby
——, *Notes on Silver Tokens of the Nineteenth Century* (1957). Seaby

Whiting, J. R., *Trade Tokens. A Social and Economic History* (1971). David & Charles

Williamson, G. C., *Trade Tokens Issued in the Seventeenth Century in England, Wales and Ireland by Corporations, Merchants, Tradesmen etc.* (1889–91, reprinted 1967). Seaby

Index